MAN A

NOTES

by
James K. Lowers, Ph.D.
Department of English
University of Hawaii

CAESAR AND CLEOPATRA

NOTES

by
Marilynn O. Harper, M.F.A.
University of Oklahoma

NEW EDITION

INCORPORATED

LINCOLN, NEBRASKA 68501

Editor

Gary Carey, M.A.
University of Colorado

Consulting Editor

James L. Roberts, Ph.D.
Department of English
University of Nebraska

ISBN 0-8220-0808-4
© Copyright 1982
by
C. K. Hillegass
All Rights Reserved
Printed in U.S.A.

Cliffs Notes, Inc.   Lincoln, Nebraska

CONTENTS

Critical Biography of Shaw 5
"MAN AND SUPERMAN"
Notes on the *Epistle Dedicatory* 12
Synopsis of *Man and Superman* 22
Act I 22
Act II 24
Act III 26
    Don Juan in Hell 28
Act IV 33
Shaw's Method and Technique 39
CHARACTERS 43
    Jack Tanner 44
    Ann Whitefield 45
    Roebuck Ramsden 48
    Octavius Robinson 48
    Violet Robinson 49
    Mrs. Whitefield 50
    Henry Straker 51
    Hector Malone, Jr. 52
    Hector Malone, Sr. 52
    Mendoza 53
    Don Juan Tenorio 54
    Dona Ana De Ulloa 55
    The Devil 56
    The Statue 57

"CAESAR AND CLEOPATRA"

The Prologue 59
An Alternative to the Prologue 61
Act I 63
Act II 66
Act III 69
Act IV 72
Act V 75
Questions for Review 78
Selected Bibliography 78

CRITICAL BIOGRAPHY OF SHAW

It is with good reason that Archibald Henderson, official biographer of his subject, entitled his work *George Bernard Shaw: Man of the Century*. Well before his death at the age of ninety-four, this famous dramatist and critic had become an institution. Among the literate, no set of initials were more widely known than G.B.S. Born on July 26, 1856, in Dublin, Ireland, Shaw survived until November 2, 1950. His ninetieth birthday in 1946 was the occasion for an international celebration, the grand old man being presented with a *festschrift* entitled *GBS 90* to which many distinguished writers contributed. A London publishing firm bought space in the *Times* to voice its greetings:

GBS

Hail to thee, blithe spirit!

Shaw was the third child and only son in a family which he once described as "shabby but genteel." His father, George Carr Shaw, was a second cousin to a baronet. For a time he was employed as a civil servant and later became a not too successful merchant. Shaw remembered especially his "alcoholic antics," for the father was a remorseful, yet unregenerated drinker. But from him the son inherited his superb comic gift. Lucinda Gurley Shaw, the mother, was the daughter of a country gentleman of Carlow. A gifted singer and music teacher, she led her son to develop a passion for music, particularly operatic. At an early age he had memorized, among others, the works of Mozart, whose fine workmanship he never ceased to admire. Somewhat later he taught himself to play the piano — in the Shavian manner.

One of the maxims in *The Revolutionist's Handbook,* appended to *Man and Superman* reads: "He who can does. He who can't teaches." Shaw, who was to insist that all art is didactic and viewed himself as a kind of teacher, had little respect for schoolmasters and formal education. First his uncle, the Reverend George Carroll, tutored him. At the age of ten he became a pupil at Wesleyan Connexional School in Dublin and later attended two other schools for short periods of time. He hated them all and declared that he learned absolutely nothing. But Shaw possessed certain qualities which are not always developed in the classroom: an acquisitive mind and the capacity for independent study. Once asked about his early education, he replied: "I can remember no time at which a page of print was not intelligible to me, and can only suppose I was born literate." He went on to add that by the age of ten he had saturated himself in Shakespeare and the Bible.

A depleted family exchequer led Shaw to accept employment as a clerk in a Land Agency when he was sixteen. He proved to be an efficient, dependable employee and was properly rewarded at intervals. But he was never satisifed with such an occupation. Determined to become a professional writer, he resigned after five years of service and joined his mother, who was then teaching music in London. The year was 1876.

During the next three years he cheerfully permitted his mother to support him and concentrated largely on trying to support himself as an author. No less than five novels came from his pen between the years 1879 and 1883. The first, *Immaturity*, remained unpublished for some fifty years; four later ones finally did make their way into print. Best known is *Cashel Byron's Profession,* the story of a prize fighter. It was quite apparent that Shaw's genius was not that of the novelist.

In 1879 Shaw was induced to accept employment in a firm promoting the new Edison telephone, his duties being those of a right-of-way agent. He detested the task of interviewing residents in the East End of London and endeavoring to get their permission for the installation of poles and equipment. A few months of such work was enough for him. In his own words, this was the last time he sinned against his nature by seeking to earn an honest living.

The year 1879 had greater significance for Shaw. He joined the Zetetical Society, a debating club, the members of which held lengthy discussions on such subjects as economics, science, and religion. Soon he found himself in demand as a speaker and a regular participant at public meetings. At one such meeting held in September, 1882, he listened spellbound to Henry George, apostle of Land Nationalization and the Single Tax. Shaw credits the American with having roused his interest in economics and social theory; theretofore he had concerned himself chiefly with the conflict between science and religion. Told that no one could do justice to George's theories without being familiar with those of Karl Marx, Shaw promptly read a French translation of *Das Kapital,* no English translation being then available. He was now converted to socialism.

The year 1884 is also a notable one in the life of Bernard Shaw (as he preferred to be called). After reading a tract entitled *Why are the Many Poor?* and learning that it was published by the Fabian Society, he appeared at the society's next meeting. The intellectual temper of the group, which included such distinguished men as Havelock Ellis, immediately attracted him. He was accepted as a member on September 5 and was elected to the Executive Committee in January. Among the debaters at the Zetetical Society was one Sidney Webb, whom he recognized as his "natural complement." He easily persuaded Webb to become a Fabian. The two with the gifted Mrs. Webb, became the pillars of the society which preached the gospel of constitutional and evolutionary socialism. Shaw's views, voiced in public park and meeting hall, are expounded at length in *The Intelligent Woman's Guide to Socialism and Capitalism* (1928); many of his ideas find a place in his dramas, including *Man and Superman.*

In the next stage of his career, Shaw emerged as a critic. Largely through the good offices of William Archer, distinguished dramatic critic now best remembered as the editor and translator of Ibsen, Shaw became a member of the reviewing staff of the *Pall Mall Gazette* in 1885. Earlier he had ghost-written some music reviews for G. L. Lee, with whom his mother long had been associated as singer and music teacher. But this new assignment provided him with his first real experience as a critic, initially as a book reviewer at two guineas per thousand words. Not long thereafter, and again through the assistance of William Archer, he added to these duties those of art critic on the widely influential *World.* Archer insisted that Shaw knew very little about art but thought that he did, which was what mattered. As for Shaw, he blandly explained that the way to learn about art was to look at pictures: he had begun doing so years earlier in the Dublin National Gallery.

This was just the beginning. When T. P. O'Connor, a leading advocate of Irish Home Rule, founded *The Star* in order to publicize his political views, Shaw was hired as a political writer in 1888. His socialistic philosophy was too extreme for O'Connor, who shifted Shaw to writing regular columns on music under the pseudonym "Corno di Bassetto." Two years later he succeeded Louis Meyer as music critic of *The World;* his lively style and often daring pronouncements won him a wide and appreciative audience. Shaw once remarked: "If you do not say a thing in an irritating way, you may just as well not say it at all." And it must be conceded that he had affiliations, at least, with what may be called the Hatchet School of Criticism. Typical is the following: "During the past month Art has suffered an unusually severe blow at the hands of the Royal Academy by the opening of the annual exhibition at Burlington House." As music critic, he once described the program given before the visiting Shah of Persia at Covent Garden as "the most extravagantly Bedlamite hotch-potch on record, even in the annals of State concerts." To paraphrase Shaw's own words, he never aimed at impartiality. He aimed at readability and individuality, and he rarely missed. Moreover, as the courageous champion of Wagner, whose music was not accepted in England, and of the neglected Mozart, Shaw distinguished himself.

Shaw's close association with William Archer was paramount in his championing of Henrik Ibsen as a new, highly original dramatist whose works represented a complete break with the popular theater of the day. "When Ibsen came from Norway," Shaw was to write, "with his characters who thought and discussed as well as acted, the theatrical heaven rolled up like a scroll." Whereas the general public, nurtured on the "well-made" romantic and melodramatic play, denounced Ibsen as a "muck-ferreting dog," Shaw saw him as a great ethical philosopher and social critic—a role which recommended itself to Shaw himself. On July 18, 1890, he read a paper on Ibsen at a meeting of the Fabian Society. Amplified, this became *The Quintessence of Ibsen* (1891). Sometimes called *The Quintessence of Shaw*, it sets forth the author's profoundest views on the function of the dramatist, who should especially concern himself with how his characters react to various social forces and who should concern himself further with a new morality based upon an examination and challenge of the conventional.

In view of what Shaw had written about Ibsen (and himself) and of his activities as a socialist exhorter, *The Widowers' Houses*, his first play, may be called characteristic. Structurally, it represents no departure from the tradition of the well-made play; that is, the action is plotted so that the key situation is exposed in the second act and the third act is devoted to its resolution. But thematically, the play was revolutionary in England. It dealt with the evils of slum-landlordism, a subject hardly calculated to regale the typical Victorian audience. Produced at J. T. Grein's Independent Theatre in London, it made a sensation because of its "daring" theme, but never was a theatrical success. Shaw was not at all discouraged. The furor delighted him. No one knew better than he the value of attracting attention. He was already at work on *The Philanderer*, an amusing but rather slight comedy of manners.

In 1894 Shaw's *Arms and the Man* enjoyed a good run at the Avenue Theatre from April 21 to July 7, and has been revived from time to time to this very day. Now the real Shaw had emerged: the dramatist who united irrepressible gaiety and complete seriousness of purpose. It has been described as "a satire on the prevailing bravura style" and sets forth the "view of romance as the great heresy to be swept from art and life," a theme which was to find its place in *Man and Superman*.

In the same year Shaw wrote *Mrs. Warren's Profession*, which became a *cause célèbre*. Shaw himself grouped it with his "Unpleasant Plays." Dealing with the economic causes of prostitution and the conflict between the prostitute mother and her daughter, it created a tumult which was kept alive for years on both sides of the Atlantic. It may well be argued that in this play he was far more the polemist than the artist, but it has its place among the provocative dramas of ideas.

The indefatigable Shaw was already at work on his first unquestionably superior play, *Candida*. First produced in 1895, it has held the boards ever since and has found its place in anthologies. Notable for effective character portrayal and the adroit use of inversions, it tells how Candida and the Reverend Morrell, widely in public demand as an advanced thinker, reached an honest and sound basis for a lasting marriage.

Early in January 1895 Shaw became the drama critic for *The Saturday Review*, edited by Frank Harris, who was wise enough to give him free rein. His essays now fill two volumes which were first published in 1931 and are indeed a valuable record of "Our Theatres in the Nineties." Sir Max Beerbohm, who succeeded Shaw in May 1898, testified as follows: "I never tire of his two volumes. He was at the very top of his genius when he wrote them." Although Shaw often had kind words to say about Oscar Wilde, Henry Arthur Jones, and others he was as outspoken and irreverent in his drama reviews as he had been in those of music; for he was determined to reform Victorian drama, to transform it into a vehicle for the dissemination of significant ideas. Characteristic are his comments on Wilde's *The Importance of Being Earnest*, surely as good a farce as there is in the language, one which Wilde himself called "a trivial comedy for serious people." Shaw joined the audience in laughing heartily at the many farcical situations, but firmly concluded that it was no more than "a silly play with a flippant wit." To Sir Henry Irving, England's premier Shakespearean actor, Shaw became practically an anathema. Long since the playwright-critic had begun a running battle with Shakespeare — at first to help win recognition for Ibsen; thereafter, in all probability, to attract attention to himself. But what especially offended him was Irving's propensity for drastic cutting of the Shakespearean text.

While working with the Fabians, Shaw met the personable Charlotte Payne-Townshend, an Irish heiress deeply concerned with the problem of social justice. He was immediately attracted to her. After she had helped him through a long illness, the two were married in 1898. She became his modest but capable critic and assistant throughout the years of their marriage.

During this period there was no surcease of play writing on Shaw's part. He completed *You Never Can Tell, The Man of Destiny,* and *The Devil's Disciple.* The last-named play, an inverted Victorian-type melodrama first acted in the United States, was an immediate success, financially and otherwise. By the turn of the century Shaw had written *Caesar and Cleopatra* and *The Admirable Bashville.* He was now the major force in the new drama of the twentieth century. Even William Archer acknowledged his supremacy. At first insisting that Shaw knew no more about plays than he did about art, Archer was completely won over by *Mrs. Warren's Profession.*

The year 1903 is especially memorable for the completion and publication of *Man and Superman.* It was first acted (without the Don Juan in Hell intermezzo which consitutes Act III) in 1905. Some twenty-three other plays were added to the Shavian canon as the century advanced toward the halfway mark. Best known among these are *Major Barbara* (1905), *Androcles and the Lion* (1912), *Pygmalion* (1912), *Heartbreak House* (1916), *Back to Methuselah* (1921), *Saint Joan* (1923). In 1930-32 the Ayot St. Lawrence Edition of his collected plays was published. Shaw's literary pre-eminence had found world-wide recognition. He refused to accept either a knighthood or the Order of Merit offered by the Crown, but in 1926 did accept the Nobel Prize for Literature. It was quite typical of him to state that the award was given to him by a grateful public because he had not published anything in that year.

Shaw had persistently rejected offers from film makers. According to one story, when importuned by Samuel Goldwyn, the well-known Hollywood producer, he replied: "The difficulty, Mr. Goldwyn, is that you are an artist and I am a business man." But later the ardor and ability of Gabriel Pascal impressed him, and he agreed to prepare the scenario of *Pygmalion* for production. The film, released in 1938, was a notable success. *Major Barbara* and *Androcles and the Lion* followed; the Irish-born dramatist had now won a much larger audience. *My Fair Lady,* a musical adapted from *Pygmalion,* opened in New Haven, Connecticut, on February 4, 1956, starring Rex Harrison and Julie Andrews. It was and remains a spectacular success.

Discussing *Macbeth,* Shaw once wrote: "I want to be thoroughly used up when I die, for the harder I work, the more I live. I rejoice in life for its own sake. Life is no 'brief candle' for me. It is a sort of splendid torch, which I have got hold of for the moment; and I want to make it burn as brightly as possible before handing it on to future generations." Life indeed was a bright torch which burned long for Bernard Shaw. Almost to the very end, when he was bed-ridden with a broken hip, he lived up to his credo. He was ninety-two years old in 1949 when *Buoyant Billions* was produced at the Malvern Festival. In the same year his highly readable *Sixteen Self Sketches* was published. He was planning the writing of still another play when he died on November 2, 1950.

NOTES ON THE *EPISTLE DEDICATORY*

In this stimulating and amusing letter addressed to Arthur Bingham Walkley, dramatic critic of *The Times,* Shaw provides, among other things, the details relating to the genesis of *Man and Superman* and an exegesis of his current philosophy and of certain dominant ideas in the play. Although Walkley had praised Shaw as "a man who can give us a refined intellectual pleasure," he did not rate his friend very highly as a dramatist. Since Shaw had been conducting a running battle against current romantic drama, Walkley playfully suggested that Shaw show how the love theme should be developed by writing a Don Juan play. And the dramatist has now complied. Aware that Walkley believed that he wrote dialectic, not drama, which (in the words of Aristotle) should be an imitation of an *action,* Shaw wittily concedes that he has the "temperament of a schoolmaster" and identifies himself as a reformer expressing his annoyance at the fact that people remain comfortable when they ought to be uncomfortable. The implication is clear: when one is comfortable he has no desire for change and thus progress is impossible. "If you don't like my preaching you must lump it," Shaw concludes. All these give some insight into Shaw's comic theory. In his *Praise of Comedy*, Mr. James Feibleman defines comedy as the "satiric criticism of the present limited historical order and a campaign for the unlimited logical order." This involves a departure from an older view which called for approval of the conventional. Shaw would have endorsed Feibleman's view. To be sure, brilliant comedies had been based on the older theory. Henri Bergson, developing his ideas of the comic chiefly with reference to the plays of Molière, insisted that such ridiculous figures as Harpagon and Tartuffe, placed themselves outside the pale of the conventional because they suffered from an inelasticity — they had become automations and thus invited derisive laughter. Shaw went further. He believed that it was not just the occasional individual who made himself ridiculous; it was the larger society, and it was the conventional itself which often was absurd. So long as it was so afflicted, society had no right to be comfortable.

Shaw dismisses current romantic plays as "childish" and insists that they are quite devoid of interest and have been "forced to deal almost exclusively with cases of sexual attraction, and yet forbidden to exhibit the incidents of that attraction or even to discuss its nature." So he has accepted Walkley's challenge; he has indeed written a Don Juan play; but it is one "in which the natural attraction of the sexes for one another is the mainspring of the action." The adjective *natural* is the significant word here. Shaw distinguishes between eroticism and sex. For him, most dramas had been concerned with the former, not the latter, which is instinctual and procreative.

Of course Shaw cannot merely rewrite the Don Juan story as it has come down in versions and variants through the centuries. The original story written by a sixteenth-century Spanish priest told how Don Juan, scion of the illustrious Tenorio family, lived a life of unbridled licentiousness and ultimately killed the governor of Seville, whose daughter he had been attempting to abduct. His sensuality having destroyed all faith in the spirit world, he then visited the tomb of the murdered man and challenged his statue to follow him to supper. The challenge was accepted; the animated statue appeared at table among the guests and carried the blaspheming skeptic to Hell. The moral, as Shaw remarks, is a monkish one: no one can escape God's inexorable justice; repent before it is too late. That will not be the text of Shaw's preaching.

It remained for Molière to give a new aspect to the character in *Don Juan, ou le Festin de Pierre* (1655). The hero, though as heartlessly depraved as in the Spanish original, loses some of the sterner elements of character and becomes more seductive and more amusing. Mozart's opera, *Don Giovanni,* the libretto of which was furnished by Da Ponte, has done more to popularize the story in Molière as distinct from the severer early Spanish form than any other setting, literary or musical, has ever received.

Shaw argues that what had attracted readers and audiences to Don Juan from the very first is not the moral lesson but Don Juan's "heroism of daring to be the enemy of God. From Prometheus to my own Devil's Disciple, such enemies have always been popular." Here we have one of the keys to Shaw's interest in the story: he too could depict a hero who was a rebel on the grand scale, but one who was an enemy of the false gods of society.

And surely Walkley knows that Shaw cannot depict Don Juan in an aristocratic society dominated by men. Not only has the middle class come into its own, but woman has become completely emancipated: "Man is no longer, like Don Juan, victor in the duel of sex...the enormous superiority of Woman's natural position in this matter is telling with greater and greater force." Here writes the man who had hailed the advent of the New Woman in his praise of Ibsen and in his own *Candida.* A modern Don Juan, Shaw continues, does not even pretend to read Ovid (*The Art of Love,* Roman classic of eroticism); he has read "Schopenhauer and Nietzsche, studied Westermarck, and is concerned for the future of the race instead of for the freedom of his own instincts."

The identification of these authors is quite significant, pointing as it does to Shaw's new approach to the sex theme in English drama. Edward Alexander Westermarck, the distinguished Finnish anthropologist who accepted the appointment as Professor of

Sociology at the University of London in 1907, is best known for his scholarly *The History of Human Marriage* and as an authority on morals. Obviously, it is the human race, not the individual, which is his prime concern. Arthur Schopenhauer (1788-1860), the famous German philosopher whose best known work is *The World as Will and Idea,* expressed many revolutionary ideas which recommended themselves to Shaw, although the latter rejected Schopenhauer's pessimism. It was the German philosopher, for example, who identified Force—Life Force, to use Shaw's term—as inner will operating independent of intellect (Shaw was to modify this); who rejected romantic love and argued that sex relates properly to the weal and woe of the species, not merely to the individual; who wrote that woman exists in the main solely for the propagation of the species and in their hearts take the affairs of the species more seriously than those of the individual. Friedrich Wilhelm Nietzsche (1844-1900) is perhaps even more widely known as an original and revolutionary philosopher who emphasized self-aggrandizement or the will to power, as the chief motivating force of both the individual and society. It was he also who saw woman as a kind of trap of the Life Force, of which she was the instinctive agent.

The modern Don Juan, Shaw continues, is anything but a profligate. He is a philosophic man, "more Hamlet than Don Juan" of tradition. At this point Shaw digresses a bit to renew his feud with Shakespeare, deploring the "mere harmonious platitude" in Hamlet's lines and the "absurd sensational incidents and physical violences of the borrowed story." The point is that Shaw believed that Shakespeare should have written more like John Bunyan, William Blake, or Shelley (who was for Shaw "a religious force"); that he should never have pandered to popular taste but should have been always the artist-philosopher. Or, to put it in other words, Shakespeare should have accepted the role of preacher.

Returning to his main subject, Shaw emphasizes his view that the modern Don Juan is not to be confused with Casanova (1725-98), that gifted Italian who is popularly identified as the prototype of the libertine. Shaw's Don Juan, then, is "a figure superficially quite unlike the hero of Mozart." But since the dramatist has not the heart to deprive Walkley of a view of the original Don Juan's nemesis, the ambulatory statue, he has resorted to a kind of trick: he has introduced into a perfectly modern three-act play a "totally extraneous act." This is the Don Juan in Hell intermezzo, which Shaw describes as "a Shavio-Socratic dialogue" and which gives Don Juan the opportunity to philosophize at great length in his talk with the lady, the Statue, and the Devil.

Returning to the discussion of the play proper, Shaw again emphasizes the fact that he has merely executed Walkley's commission, the dramatization of "sexual attraction to wit." And in doing so, he has been steadfastly realistic: he has not adulterated the product with "aphrodisiacs" nor "diluted it with water." All this, of course, is another hit at the current romantic drama which was an anathema to Shaw. His is a story of modern London life, where the ordinary man strives to maintain his position as a gentleman, and the ordinary woman is concerned with marriage. After all, the law of nature is involved: money means nourishment, which is man's first concern; marriage means children, which are woman's prime interest.

Shaw comes pretty close to reducing the average human being to an amoeba at this point in his discussion of these two basic drives. Or, perhaps more accurately, he shows the influence of the relatively new naturalism, according to which the instinctual was emphasized and sex and hunger identified as the ultimate sources of human behavior. Early and late he had been interested in the institution of marriage. Some of his ideas found expression in his fifth novel, *An Unsocial Socialist* (1884), in which Sidney Trefusis, is an outspoken rationalist like Jack Tanner in *Man and Superman*. He had been especially influenced by Samuel Butler, whose *The Way of All Flesh* is a keenly satiric criticism of English family life in the middle classes. But what Shaw is leading up to immediately is an endorsement of Socialism. The prosaic Englishman, he states, is like all prosaic people — stupid. Such a person does not realize that the present system where at all costs every man wants to be rich and every woman to be married "must produce a ruinous development of poverty, celibacy, prostitution, infant mortality, adult degeneracy, and everything men most dread." Socialism would make possible a highly scientific social organization which would eliminate all these evils.

Back to the play. It will deal with sexual attraction, not nutrition. The serious business of sex is left by men to women, who let men concern themselves with nourishment. Shaw tacitly denies that there is anything revolutionary in this: in Shakespeare's plays the women always take the initiative, and the pursuing female is found in joyous and dark comedies alike. This is the "Shakespearean law" in the realm of sex, so says Shaw. Thus he makes clear the basic plot line of *Man and Superman:* the tragi-comic love chase of man by woman.

The dramatist concedes that some friends who had heard him read the play were shocked at woman's unscrupulousness in her pursuit and capture of man. They should realize that woman is doing no more than following the law of nature; if she did otherwise there would be an end of the human race. Shaw pokes fun at man's hypocrisy and capacity for deluding himself—his view of woman as the lesser man, his "speaking of Woman's 'sphere' with condescension, even with chivalry, as if the kitchen and nursery were less important than the office in the city." Among the unrealistic and the uninformed, it is assumed that woman must wait motionless until some man proposes marriage to her. If she does wait motionless, it is as the spider waits for the fly!

Shaw next explains why great literature and works of art so often treat sex unrealistically. If ordinary men produced the really superior works of art, those works would express fear of predatory woman, rather than love of her illusory beauty. But the man of genius is free of the tyranny of sex. When he is young it means for him pleasure, excitement, and knowledge; when he is old, it is a source of contemplative tranquility. His purpose, like that of woman, is impersonal and irresistible. Books produced by these artists present no true picture of the world; they reveal "only the self-consciousness of certain abnormal people who have specific artistic talent and temperament." So it is that the scripture and great art works do not treat love scientifically, but deal with "romantic nonsense, erotic ecstasy, or the stern asceticism of satiety." But among the exceptionally gifted, there are those who are normal and who have no private ax to grind; these are the ones who drive towards truth.

According to Shaw, the fact that woman is the pursuer has important political implications, for democracy, "the last refuge of cheap misgovernment," will ruin us if rapine were not repressed and importunity discouraged. He then takes a look at the political situation in Britain, that "tight but parochial little island." When he and Walkley were born, Aristocracy and Plutocracy still ran the government; the country was run by a selected class into which one had to be born. Now the commercial class, the membership in which is determined by money, has its new share of political power. And all this has taken place at a time when Great Britain has become a Commonwealth of Nations and is witnessing the partition of all of Africa and perhaps all of Asia. Can anyone believe that the new class will measure up to the great responsibility which faces the nation? Voters show no more intelligence in the polling booths than they do when attending the public theaters. Quoting Edmund Burke, Shaw concludes that the nation now is under "the hoofs of the swinish multitude."

This statement may come as a surprise to those who assumed that an avowed Socialist must love the common people. Shaw certainly did not hate them; he simply had no confidence in their ability to rule effectively. He has no more confidence in formal education, in Progress, or in Heredity. "Any pamphleteer," Shaw writes, "can shew the way to better things; but when there is no will there is no way...Progress can do nothing but make the most of us all as we are..." In rejecting Heredity, Shaw specifically refers to an hereditary ruling class such as the aristocracy or the new commercial class. Direfully he predicts that, unless an electorate of capable critics is found, modern civilization will collapse as did those of Rome and Egypt. In his intensity he voices sentiments to be found in the first two lines of Wordsworth's well-known sonnet which was written a century earlier:

The world is too much with us late and soon,
Getting and spending we lay waste our powers....

British newspapers and melodramas bluster about imperial destiny, but the eyes of the populace are on the American millionaire. Since an American millionaire has a prominent role in *Man and Superman,* Shaw's remarks are of special interest.

At this point one might conclude that the dramatist was in a state of complete pessimism. One cannot deny that the Fabian Shaw had suffered disillusionment in political theory as the source of man's achievement. But he remained idealistic and optimistic and dismissed political change as the solution to social problems in preparation for the setting forth of a new solution.

Shaw next reassures Walkley: he has not put all this "tub-thumping" into his comedy. Only his modern Don Juan, Jack Tanner, appears as a political pamphleteer; and his views are recorded in *The Revolutionist's Handbook,* an appendix to the play. Shaw is not one of those romancers who proclaims the superiority of his hero and then denies his audience access to the hero's works. In the handbook is to be found the "politics of the sex question" as Shaw conceived Don Juan's ancestors to understand them. He admits that, at the dramatic moment, Tanner speaks for him. Aware that many people naively believe that there is only one absolutely right point of view, Shaw offers a word of caution. No one who is such an absolutist can be a dramatist or anything else. His point is that truth often remains an illusive thing and that an issue would not be an issue unless honest and reasonable people differed strongly about it.

Shaw anticipates possible criticism. Since he is an artist, he can never grasp the common man's view of sex. Had he not himself insisted that the artist is free from its tyranny? Is it not therefore presumptuous for him to write a Don Juan play? Not at all. First it was Walkley who urged him to do so. More important, his treatment of the subject may have validity for the artist; it may amuse the amateur; it may be intelligible and suggestive to the Philistine. "Every man who records his illusions is providing data for the genuinely scientific psychology," he concludes. In making such a statement of substance and pith Shaw is sufficiently modest. But immediately he assures Walkley that what he writes is far beyond the intelligence of the public with its "simple romantic head.'"He does not need to be told that this long epistle dedicatory and the dream of Don Juan in Act III cannot be produced in a popular theater. "As for me, what I have always wanted is a pit of philosophers; and this is a play for such." In other words his play indeed is a comedy of ideas; it bears the subtitle "A Comedy and a Philosophy."

Shaw makes his acknowledgement of sources and influences in his creation of leading characters in *Man and Superman*. From the works of Arthur Conan Doyle, best remembered as the author of the Sherlock Holmes stories, he "stole" the character of the brigand-poetaster; that is, Mendoza, leader and favorite orator of the brigands encamped in the Spanish Sierra Nevada. He took over Leporella, servant to Don Giovanni in Mozart's opera, but changed him into Enry Straker, a representative of the new engineering and mechanic class which H. G. Wells had predicted would ultimately dominate in a society dependent upon the machine. Shaw also points out that in *The Admirable Crichton,* the dramatic success of the year 1902, Sir James Matthew Barrie had anticipated him by creating a servant who is better informed than his master. In his knowledge of women and machines, so Enry Straker is. Shaw had high praise for Barrie's play, for it too is a drama of ideas.

Under the leadership of Mendoza, the brigands introduced at the beginning of Act III have formed a League of the Sierra. Shaw explains that the idea came to him when he recalled that a certain West Indian Colonial Secretary, impressed by Sidney Webb's encyclopedic knowledge, suggested that Webb "form himself into a company for the benefit of the shareholders." Shaw refers to the Colonial Secretary, Webb, and himself as the "Fabian Three Musketeers."

Octavius, the dramatist states, comes straight from Mozart. In the opera, it will be recalled, he is Don Ottavio, who is engaged to Donna Ana; in Shaw's play Octavius is romantically in love with Ann, but is not her fiancé. Ann herself, Shaw continues, was suggested by the fifteenth-century morality play, *Everyman.* He had asked himself why there should not be an Everywoman. Ann, he concludes, is just that, but every woman is not Ann. By this Shaw means that Ann, instinctively aware of her destiny as one upon whom the survival and future of the human race depends, is the pursuer in the love game; but imbued as she is with Vital Force and a high degree of perspicuity she is not to be taken as the prototype of every woman.

Declaring that the unknown author of *Everyman* was "no mere artist, but an artist-philosopher," Shaw pays his tribute to these superior beings and inveighs once more against melodrama and romance. Among his heroes are Mozart, Bunyan, Blake, Hogarth, and Turner; and he claims literary kinship with Goethe, Shelley, Schopenhauer, Wagner, Ibsen, William Morris, Tolstoy, and Nietzsche. Shaw concedes that he does read Shakespeare and Dickens, but finds them limited because "their pregnant observations and demonstrations are not co-ordinated into any philosophy or religion." There follows a rather detailed discussion of various characters in Shakespeare's plays and Dickens' novels, and a no less detailed eulogy of the writers to whom he has given the accolade of the artist-philosopher. In this portion of the epistle, Shaw is as downright as ever. He decries Dickens' "sentimental assumptions," which he finds to be "violently contradicted by his observations"; he flatly states that to Shakespeare the world was "a great 'stage of fools' on which he was utterly bewildered." In contrast, the Shavian artist-philosophers from Bunyan to Nietzsche saw life realistically and portrayed it courageously. The reader may be a bit surprised to find that, according to Shaw, *Pilgrim's Progress* is "A consistent attack on morality and respectability" and that Nietzsche's philosophical writing has close affinities with it. What he is getting at is the idea that the greatest writers avoid "Tappertitian romance" (the reference is to Sim Tappertit, the would-be-lover of Dolly Varden in Dickens' *Barnaby Rudge*) and "the garish splendors and alcoholic excitements" of melodrama. Above all the great writer is one who has the courage to attack the conventional and what passes for morality.

Shaw concludes, at long last, by stating that for art's sake alone he "would not face the toil of writing a single sentence." "Art for art's sake" is the doctrine which holds that the aim of art should be creation and the perfection of technical expression rather than the service of a moral, political, or didactic end. Adumbrated by Coleridge and given early expression in Edgar Allan Poe's *The Poetic Principle,* the doctrine had been evolving ever since the Romantic period and was widely popular at the time Shaw was writing. Little wonder that he should reject it, for Shaw advertises the fact that he is a man with a message. But he is wise enough to know that he cannot gain or hold an audience unless he can present it entertainingly.

SYNOPSIS OF *MAN AND SUPERMAN*

ACT I

The setting is a study in Portland Place, London. On stage is Roebuck Ramsden, a rather elderly man of affluence and affairs. Octavius Robinson, a young poet, is announced by the maid. He appears dressed in an elegant suit of mourning. As Ramsden consoles him, the audience learns that Octavius' benefactor and friend, Mr. Whitefield is dead. Ramsden is confident that he will be the one who will serve as guardian of Whitefield's daughters, Ann and Rhoda, and he expresses his hope that Ann and Octavius will marry. Octavius can think of nothing which would make him happier. As they discuss this matter, Ramsden warns the young poet against the latter's friend, John Tanner, author of the notorious *Revolutionist's Handbook*. Ramsden prides himself on being an advanced thinker and liberal but regards Tanner as an immoral person. If Ramsden indeed is to be the guardian of the lovely Ann, he will see to it that Tanner is kept away from her.

At this point the object of Ramsden's disapproval appears. Jack Tanner, an attractive and obviously superior young man, is in a state of near-panic. As he excitedly informs Ramsden, both he and the latter have been appointed by Whitefield's will to act as Ann's guardians. Ironically, Tanner, to whom Ramsden is hopelessly old-fashioned, was responsible for his own appointment, one which he dreads. He had advised Mr. Whitefield to team Ramsden up with a younger man, not dreaming that he would be Whitefield's choice. He pleads with Ramsden to get him out of this predicament, arguing that Ann is anything but the weak, dutiful young woman. He sees her as wilful and hypocritical and declares that she will "commit every crime a respectable woman can." Ramsden himself states emphatically that he will refuse to act as guardian with Tanner. But the younger man prophesies that neither one of them will escape the obligations which have been forced upon them. Octavius is as appalled at Tanner's unflattering description of Ann as an unscrupulous siren as Ramsden is at Tanner's political views. To him she is a goddess; nor can anything that

Tanner says convince him that she is not divine. For the naive Octavius she is the "reality of romance."

Now Ann makes her appearance. Shaw describes her as "perfectly ladylike, graceful, and comely, with ensnaring eyes and hair." What sets her apart from other beautiful women is her abundant vitality. With her is Mrs. Whitefield, her mother, a little woman certainly devoid of such vitality, one who wears an expression of "muddled shrewdness." Playing her role of the dutiful and helpless daughter, Ann listens to Ramsden, who tells her that Tanner and he have been named as joint guardians and trustees of the late Mr. Whitefield's two daughters. Tanner's prophesy is soon justified. Ann will not violate her father's will; both Ramsden, whom she calls "Granny," and Jack must serve.

Ramsden, who had left the stage while Octavius and Jack express their markedly contrasting views of Ann, returns with "terrible news." Octavius' sister Violet is about to become an unmarried mother. All but Tanner are greatly shocked. He declares that the girl should be congratulated on "the fulfillment of her highest purpose and greatest function — to increase, multiply, and replenish the earth." It is Ramsden especially who expresses the conventional attitude: Violet is the victim of "a rascal...a libertine, a villain worse than a murderer" who is in their very midst! When he expresses his suspicions of Tanner, whom he describes as "a man of notoriously loose principles," Tanner adroitly points out that suspicion clings to Ramsden as well.

For the first time alone together on the stage, Ann and Jack converse. The audience learns that the two had known each other since childhood and that Jack had once declared his love for her. She does admit that once, when he had pretended to be in love with another girl, she had violated Jack's confidence; she had told the girl that Jack had informed her of the attachment. Tanner states that, as a result of his experience, he has come to believe moral passion to be the only real passion; no romance for him now. The entire episode is replete with interesting Shavian ideas which will be discussed later. What especially is made clear is that Ann indeed is the active one in the love game. As Tanner says, "I never feel safe with you: there is a devilish charm — or no: a subtle interest...."

Ramsden and Octavius come back with Miss Ramsden, a hard-headed spinster who is determined that Violet must leave the house at once since she apparently wished to meet her betrayer again. Violet herself enters. She is quite self-possessed and obviously impenitent. When Tanner eloquently voices his approval of her, she turns upon him and vehemently repudiates his compliments. In so doing, Violet is forced to reveal the fact that she has been secretly married and is not a fallen woman at all.

ACT II

The setting is the carriage drive in the park of the house near Richmond. Jack Tanner, dressed in the contemporary costume for motoring, is watching his chauffeur, Henry Straker, who is repairing the automobile. The conversation between the two reveals that Enry (as he is usually called) is one of the new type of servants, one who is quite aware of his superiority in the world of machines. Jack Tanner is undoubtedly right when he wryly observes that the master has become the slave to the car and the chauffeur. Tanner tells Enry that one Mr. Malone, an American gentleman, is driving Octavius down in a new American steam car. Enry expresses his disappointment that he could not have had a race with them but is consoled by the news that both cars will be used for transporting the entire group, which will include Octavius, Violet, Ann, Rhoda, and Jack himself. He is incredulous, however, when he is told that Ann will not ride in Jack's car.

Octavius returns and an amusing colloquy follows when Tanner explains Enry's status as the New Man, a member of the class-conscious engineers. Not disrespectful, the chauffeur is anything but differential. He is aware that he does know more about machines — and women — than does his master.

Left alone with Tanner, Octavius solicits his sympathy. He had proposed to and been rejected by Ann. Jack insists that he has not been rejected at all and that Ann merely is not through playing with him. She is the pursuer, he argues, and Octavius is her marked-out victim. But poor love-sick Octavius rejects this counsel as only another sample of Jack's "eternal shallow cynicism." When Tanner learns that Ann had reproached his friend for not getting his permission to approach her, he pronounces blessings on the two and wishes them happiness. But he adds that Ann is really as free to choose as is Octavius. There follows a disputation on the subject of love as viewed by Tanner and Octavius respectively. When Straker reappears, the conversation shifts to Enry's preoccupation with motor racing.

Octavius gives Jack a note from Rhoda Whitefield, who has written that her elder sister Ann had forbidden her to go on the motor trip with Tanner and even to be in his company at any time on the grounds that he is "not a fit person for a young girl." Octavius sides with Ann, arguing that Jack's views are certainly not proper for the development of a young girl's mind and character.

Ann appears with the news that poor Rhoda cannot join the motoring party because she has one of her headaches. Jack is vastly amused; he has trapped Ann in a lie from which he is sure she cannot extricate herself. But Ann succeeds in doing just that. After sending Octavius to look after his American friend, she explains that she had been only the dutiful daughter carrying out her mother's instructions — another lie, of course. This provides Tanner with the cue for delivering a tirade on the tyranny of mothers and to challenge Ann to show her independence by joining him on a continental motor trip. To his chagrin, she promptly agrees to do so. After all, she explains, no impropriety would be involved, for Jack is her guardian and stands in her father's place.

Mrs. Whitefield arrives, accompanied by Hector Malone, the young American, and followed by Ramsden and Octavius. It is Jack's hope that Mrs. Whitefield will absolutely forbid Ann to go to the Continent with him. He is told that she has not the slightest objection — why should she object? Indeed, Mrs. Whitefield says that she had intended to ask Jack to take Rhoda out for a ride occasionally. So he learns that Ann had lied again. "Abyss beneath abyss of perfidy!" he exclaims. Ann hastily introduces Hector to

26

Jack in order to divert attention from this outburst. In conversation with Tanner and Octavius, Hector reveals his devotion to Violet and is warned that she is a married woman, the identity of her husband unknown. Hector, the soul of chivalry, says that he will respect the lady's wishes but cannot understand why a husband should forbid his wife to reveal his identity. All this leads to a discussion of womanhood and marriage, Tanner as usual voicing unorthodox opinions. Hector asks to have a few words in private with Violet.

Alone on stage, the two exchange kisses, and the audience then learns definitely that they are married. The motivation for their secrecy was the fact that Hector's millionaire father was set on having his son marry a member of the aristocracy, someone with "a handle to her name." Hector urges Violet to let him announce their marriage publicly even if his father disinherits him. But Violet will have none of such "nonsense." Hector must not be romantic about money, she states; she has no intention of facing a struggle and poverty. When Hector says that he can borrow money and then go to work, she is appalled: "Do you want to spoil our marriage?" The young American remains worried about having to live a lie, especially after Jack Tanner had argued that marriage had not ennobled Violet's unknown husband. To Violet, Jack is a hateful beast, but the tolerant Hector is sure that all he needs is the love of a good woman.

Tanner returns with Straker as Violet and her husband leave to inspect the steam car. Jack and Enry discuss the continental trip. In the course of their conversation, the perspicacious chauffeur tells his master that Octavius has no chance of marrying Ann and that it is Jack himself she is after. Tanner is horrified at the thought that he is "the bee, the spider, the marked-down victim" Ann is bent on capturing. Seeking escape, he calls upon Enry to set a new motoring record to get far across the Continent and out of Ann's reach.

ACT III

It is evening, and the setting is that of a natural amphitheatre in the Spanish Sierras. A group of about a dozen men recline about a dying campfire, while another serves as lookout on the adjacent rise of ground. These are an international band of brigands dedicated to stopping motor cars and robbing the occupants in order "to secure a more equitable distribution of the wealth." Their leader, a man with a fine voice and ready wit, is Mendoza. His followers include a bullfighter ruined by drink, at least one Frenchman, cockney Englishmen, and Americans. All are in their early thirties, except for one who is dressed like a broken-down English gentleman and who is anywhere from ten to twenty years older than the others; he is described as the respectable member of the group.

While waiting for victims, the brigands resume their evening debates on Anarchists and Social-Democrats. Present are one Anarchist and three Social-Democrats, making possible a lively discussion. But the others describe themselves as gentlemen and Christians. Mendoza presides with wit and skill, controlling the various speakers when they become too intense and excited. The debate is interrupted by the sound of an approaching motor car. The brigands have made the necessary preparations: nails have been strewn on the road to puncture tires; one brigand stands ready to use his rifle if the nails should fail. They do not. The car is forced to stop, and its occupants, Jack Tanner and his chauffeur, are brought in as prisoners.

Tanner accepts his capture good-naturedly. When Mendoza introduces himself as President of the League of the Sierra and states that he lives by robbing the rich, Jack identifies himself as a gentleman who lives by robbing the poor. Thus a common bond is established between the two. In view of the exchange between Enry Straker and the brigands, it is quite understandable that the chauffeur wonders whether he and his master are enjoying a trip in the mountains or attending a Socialist meeting.

Mendoza, the soul of dignity and courtesy, dismisses his followers, and announces that in Spain one puts off business until the next day. All can now relax; there will be no talk of ransom. In response to Tanner's questions and to Enry's occasional remarks, the brigand leader first talks of Socialism and then tells his life story. He, the President, had once been a successful waiter and had been driven to become a brigand by disappointment in love. No, the lady was not an Earl's daughter; she was far more attractive than the daughters of the English peerage. Moreover, if she had not been "a woman of the people" he would have scorned her. Alas, she had rejected him because he was a Jew. She had been employed by a Jewish family and had become convinced that Jews considered Gentiles, especially English Gentiles, to be dirty in their habits. When Straker recalls that his sister had once been a cook in a Jewish family, the dramatic coincidence, as Tanner calls it, is revealed. Mendoza's inamorata is Louisa, sister of Straker. Mendoza had heard a great deal about Enry, who was Louisa's favorite brother. But Straker is anything but pleased to hear a brigand tell of his love for the girl. At one point Tanner has to intervene to prevent an attempt at physical violence. Things quiet down and Enry joins the other brigands in sleep. Mendoza and Jack continue their discussion, the brigand revealing his propensity for poetry and for paraphrasing Shakespeare. Tanner solemnly advises him to give up his romantic pose and to renounce Louisa, stating that he is "sacrificing his career to a monomania." But Mendoza will not follow this counsel, for the mountains made one dream of beautiful women; indeed "this is a strange country for dreams."

When Tanner lies down and composes himself for sleep, the brigand reads him an original love lyric addressed to Louisa Straker, but Jack is asleep before he has finished.

Don Juan in Hell

The darkness deepens. The scene dissolves into an omnipresent nothing, and then somewhere there is the beginning of a pallor. To the accompaniment of eerie music a man, incorporeal but visible, is identified. He raises his head at the sound of the music, the strains of which are Mozartian. But the music fades away, extinguished by wailings from uncanny wind instruments, and the man slumps dejectedly. He is a Spanish nobleman of the fifteenth-sixteenth centuries—Don Juan himself. Oddly enough, he bears a resemblance to Tanner. Even the names of the two are alike: Juan Tenorio—Jack Tanner. An old crone wanders into the void, obviously lost. In the conversation between her and the Spaniard, the audience learns that she is a newcomer, one who had just died that morning. Understandably, she is appalled and incredulous when Don Juan tells her that she is in Hell; she had expected confidently to be translated to Heaven or at least to Purgatory. Had she not been a lady and a faithful daughter of the Church who regularly went to confession? Don Juan assures her that there are many good people in Hell. What of himself? she asks. To her consternation she learns that he was a murderer, although he later qualifies this self-indictment, explaining that he had killed his man in a duel. When Don Juan again assures her that she is in the realm of the damned, the woman laments the fact that she had wasted so many opportunities for wickedness. But she is still incredulous. Why does she feel no pain? The Spaniard explains that the wicked are always comfortable in Hell and her presence cannot be a mistake. He concedes that he is not comfortable because Hell bores him beyond belief. But then, he goes on to say, by implication, that he had not been really wicked. He explains the circumstances of the duel. His opponent had presented himself as an outraged father defending his daughter's honor and had tried to assassinate Don Juan. Actually the latter had only fallen foolishly in love with the daughter, who screamed when he proclaimed his love for her.

The old woman insists that, like all men, Don Juan was a libertine and murderer. Her own father had been slain under the identical circumstances. It had been her duty to scream, and her father's honor demanded that he attack her would-be lover. Hell, Don Juan explains, is the reward of duty. It is the home of honor, duty, justice, and the rest of the seven deadly virtues; for all the wickedness on earth is done in their name.

After discussing her status as a subject of the Devil, Don Juan tells the woman that she may assume any age she wants. She chooses to become twenty-seven and immediately is so radiantly attractive that she could almost be mistaken for Ann Whitefield. The amazed Don Juan greets her as Dona Ana de Ulloa, the young woman with whom he had had the affair which led to the duel. "You who slew my father! even here you pursue me," exclaims Ana. But Don Juan protests that he does not. She is delighted to learn that her father may visit them. When Ana asks if Don Juan had really loved her, he impatiently asks her not to talk of love: the occupants of Hell are always talking about its beauty, its holiness, its spirituality, and the like; yet they really know nothing about it.

The sound of music is heard. Don Juan recognizes it as Mozart's statue music and informs Ana that her father is about to appear. Earlier he had explained that the father often visited Hell because Heaven bored him. And the living statue of the Commander of Calatrava indeed enters. The father had chosen to retain the sculptured form because he had been admired so much more in marble than in the flesh. He does not recognize Ana; in fact he cannot immediately remember the name of his daughter and requests her to regard him as a fellow creature, not as a father. After all, he had died at the age of 64, she at 80. Ana is horrified to hear her father lauding the advantages of existence in Hell: "Hell...is a place where you have nothing to do but amuse yourself," he concludes—and Don Juan sighs as he hears these words. The Statue has decided to become a citizen of Hell, renouncing the dull and uncomfortable Heaven. At a wave of his hand, music once more is heard; but this time the Mozartian chords are grotesquely mixed with strains from Gounod's *Faust*. The Devil makes his appearance dramatically. Curiously, he looks very much like the brigand leader, Mendoza. He welcomes the Statue and dwells enthusiastically on the infernal preoccupation with joy, love, happiness, and beauty. In contrast to the Statue, Don Juan is nauseated by all this. When the Statue announces the fact that he has left Heaven for good, the Devil is elated. And since the Devil and Don Juan never see eye to eye, he urges first the Statue and then Ana to talk the Spaniard into going to Heaven. He expounds at some length on the great gulf between Heaven and Hell, speaking as an authority since he had been resident in both places. Hell is devoted to the pursuit of happiness and the cultivation of the tender emotions; Heaven is coldly intellectual. Don Juan finds Hell to be the abode of those filled with romantic illusions; he wishes to devote himself to contemplation and especially to assist in the great work of helping life to struggle upward, for he has abiding faith in man's potential. When he eulogizes man as the highest miracle of organization yet attained by life despite a limited mentality which remains to be developed, the Devil decries man as a destructive creature, one who is a bungler in the arts of peace. But Don Juan is unperturbed. He argues that the Devil's mistake is to take man at man's own evaluation of himself. In his long discourse on man's destiny, Don Juan declares that the great object of the Life Force is intellect — the evolution of the philosophic man. History has shown that man can be moved by great ideas — witness the force of Christianity. Life Force can and must move him to strive upward toward the ideal of the philosophic.

When Ana introduces the subject of women in relation to men, Don Juan is no less emphatic. He explains that, as woman sees it, man's role is to get bread for her children. Woman instinctively knows that her great mission is to bear children. "Sexually, Woman is Nature's contrivance for perpetuating its highest achievement. Sexually, Man is Woman's contrivance for fulfilling Nature's behest in the most economical way." But Man's numerical strength and superfluous energy had led him to be discontented with mere self-reproduction; he has created civilization and has done so without consulting Woman, Don Juan concludes. The Devil has his own unflattering view of man-made civilization, and the Spaniard admits that it is far from being a success. But his point is that, since Life makes a "continual effort not only to maintain itself but to achieve higher and higher organization and complete self-consciousness," only battles have been lost, not the larger conflict. Life is a force which has made and is making attempts to build itself into higher and higher individuals as its strives toward godhead. Life has been "driving at brains" through which Man can attain not only self-consciousness but self-understanding.

The Statue has little respect for brains; he has found that most of his pleasures do not bear thinking about. To this remark, Don Juan replies that that is why intellect is so unpopular, but that it is an absolute necessity to the survival of the Life Force. It follows that the philosophic man is the only man who has ever attained happiness and who has ever been universally respected; all others are tedious failures. To support his argument, Don Juan discusses doctors of medicine, doctors of divinity, and the Artist with his delightful love lyrics and paintings. He concedes that the Artist (romantic man) has indeed led him into the worship of Woman; but thanks to his social rank and wealth he had not remained a victim of romantic illusions. He had found that Woman, motivated by instinct, was always the relentless pursuer of Man.

From his experiences, Don Juan had become convinced that the Life Force recognizes marriage only as its own contrivance for securing the greatest number of children, and that it cares nothing for "honor, chastity, and all the rest of your moral figments." Indeed, he states, marriage is the most licentious of human institutions; thus its popularity. Both Ana and her father are shocked at this statement. In defense of marriage, Ana argues that it is an institution which populates the world, whereas debauchery does not. Juan replies that the day is coming when the prudent, the seekers after worldly success, the worshippers of art and love will find the device of sterility to oppose the Life Force. But, the Spaniard continues, before that process of sterilization becomes more than a clearly foreseen possibility, the reaction will begin. The great central purpose of breeding the race to "heights now deemed superhuman: that purpose now hidden in a mephitic cloud of love and romance and prudery and fastidiousness, will break through into clear sunlight as a purpose no longer to be confused with the gratification of personal fancies, the impossible realization of boys' and girls' dreams of bliss, or the need of older people for companionship or money." The colloquy between Don Juan and the Statue which follows serves amusingly to illustrate the fancies and dreams just referred to.

When the Devil tells Don Juan that Hell offers him all that he had sought in life and nothing which repelled him, the Spaniard becomes most eloquent. Hell offers only disappointments to him. "I tell you that as long as I can conceive something better than myself I cannot be easy unless I am striving to bring it into existence or clearing the way for it. That is the law of my life." In a word, the Life Force works within him, with its "incessant aspiration to higher organization, wider, deeper, intenser self-consciousness, and clearer self-understanding," all pointing to the ultimate emergence of the Superman.

The Devil's repeated reference to his religion of love and beauty only disgusts Don Juan, and when he learns that there are no artistic people in Heaven he is anxious to leave. In response to his question of how to get there, the Statue replies: "The frontier between Heaven and Hell is only the difference between two ways of looking at things; any road will take you across." Don Juan departs.

The Devil warns the Statue not to become a pursuer of Superman like Don Juan; it is dangerous, for it leads to "an indiscriminate contempt for the human." Ana asks where she can find Superman and is told that he is not yet in existence. "Then," she exclaims, "my work is not yet done. I believe in the Life to come." Addressing her words to the universe, she continues: "A father, a father for superman." Ana disappears into the void, and the scene reverts to the Sierra.

It is now the morning after. The brigands are aroused by their sentry's announcement of an approaching automobile accompanied by two armored cars filled with soldiers. Ann, Violet, Hector Malone, Ramsden, and (a bit later) Octavius enter. Ann makes straight for Jack Tanner. Hector tells Jack that she had tracked him at every stopping place — "She is a regular Sherlock Holmes." "The Life Force! I am lost," exclaims the newly found Tanner. Thanks to him, Mendoza and his followers escape arrest. Jack identifies them as his escorts, not his captors. In their respective ways, the brigands manifest their gratitude — all but the Anarchist, who defies the State with folded arms.

ACT IV

The setting now is the garden in an expensive and pretentious villa in Granada. Enry Straker enters with an elderly Irishman. The chauffeur had been asked to deliver a note to Hector at the latter's hotel. He was and still is confused by the fact that this stranger had been identified as Hector Malone, but had complied with the request to bring him along to the villa when told that "it's all right." Now he learns that the Irishman does not even know Violet Robinson's name. Violet enters, and the Irishman identifies himself as Hector Malone, Sr. (hereafter referred to as Malone to distinguish him from his son, Hector, Jr.). Throughout this first part of the scene, there is an amusing exchange between Enry and Malone on the subject of their respective dialects. Violet apologizes for any rudeness of which the confident Straker may have been guilty: "But what can we do? He is our chauffeur." A man of his mechanical skill is indispensable; all are dependent upon him.

The note had made Malone aware of his son's deep interest in some woman unknown to him; now he is told that Hector wants to marry Violet. He tells her that his son "will not have a rap" from him if his son does so because he has other plans. Malone concedes that Violet is an amiable and excellent young lady but, like his son, too romantic to be concerned with money. And he is staggered when Violet calmly states that she is not that foolish and that Hector must have money. Then he must work for it, Malone retorts. Work! There is no use having money if you have to work — it's nonsense, Violet replies coolly. But she almost loses her control when Malone advises her not to marry on the strength of such a belief. Is not her social position as good as Hector's, she next asks? The father states that his son's social position is exactly what he chooses to buy for him, and he makes it clear that he is dead-set on having Hector marry the daughter of an aristocrat. He concedes that he would not object if his son had chosen to marry a barefooted Irish girl as his own grandmother had been. Under such circumstances Malone would not have denied the young man financial help since the expenditure involved "social profit." But if Hector married Violet things would be "just like they are"; that is, he would remain middle class.

When Violet observes that many of her relatives would object to her marrying the grandson of a peasant and adds that there is obviously prejudice on both sides, Malone cannot help respecting her as "a pretty straightforward downright sort of young woman." Yet he remains firm: "I want no middle class properties and no middle class woman for Hector." The subsequent discussion about what the father should do for the son and what Violet could for him is interrupted by Hector's arrival, much to Violet's annoyance since she wanted more time to win over Malone to her point of view. Hector, playing the role of the complete man of honor, is indignant with his father for having opened the letter: "That's disawnerable." But Violet, dreading a scene, urges him to be reasonable, for Malone's name *was* on the envelope.

As father and son mutely glare at each other, Tanner, Ramsden, Octavius, and Ann come in. Ramsden is solicitous about Violet and Tanner about Hector, since both had claimed to be indisposed and thus unable to join the others on a visit to the Alhambra. When Violet asks her husband to introduce his father to the new arrivals, Hector bluntly refuses: "He is no father of mine." She implores the two not to make a scene as the astonished Ann and Octavius withdraw. Violet can only look on "in helpless annoyance as her husband soars to higher and higher moral eminences without the least regard to the old man's millions." Tanner complicates the matter by letting the cat out of the bag. Malone learns that Violet is already married and assumes that his son has been pursuing a married woman. "You've picked up the habit of the British aristocracy, have you?" he almost shouts into his son's ear. So Hector has no alternative but to avow his marriage to Violet. "She's married a beggar," says the crushed Malone. But the son rejects the appellation; he is now a Working Man, having just started to earn his living that very afternoon. He is done with remittances from a man who insults his wife. The romantic Octavius is moved almost to tears by the apparent nobility of Hector's declaration of independence and begs to be allowed to shake his hand. Violet also is on the verge of tears, but not for the same reason. "Oh, don't be an idiot, Tavey," she exclaims in vexation.

When both Tanner and Octavius generously offer to help Hector get a good start, Malone changes his tune, now jealous that anyone but him should assist his son. He urges Hector not to be rash and makes abject apologies to Violet, describing her as just the wife his son wants. So all seems well that has ended well for the newly-weds. But Hector, still presenting himself as the man of high principles is determined to be independent of his father, who urges Violet to bring the young man to his senses. At this point he readily accepts her advice to do nothing without consulting her and eagerly gives her a thousand-dollar bill, Hector's "bachelor allowance." As Tanner observes the subservience of this multi-millionaire, "one of the master spirits of the age," he wonders whether he will ever be reduced to such a state by a woman. Ramsden states that the sooner he is the better for him.

After Violet leaves, Malone is elated. "That'll be a grand woman for Hector. I wouldn't exchange her for ten duchesses," he exclaims. In the conversation between Malone, Tanner, and Ramsden it is revealed that the millionnaire's investment in Mendoza, Limited, about which he knows nothing, had brought him to Granada. Jack informs him that Mendoza is a man who is thoroughly commercial and promises to take Malone to him. The Irishman and Ramsden depart. Tanner calls to Octavius, who is walking in the garden with Ann, and tells him that his sister's father-in-law is "a financier of brigands." He hurries after Malone and Ramsden.

Octavius now tries once more to win the hand of the girl he worships. But Ann tells him that she has no voice in the matter because her mother is determined that she will marry Jack. For a moment Tavy believes that his friend has been false to him in urging him not to marry Ann; but she insists that such is not the case, adding that Jack does not really know his own mind. She then tells Tavy that, not only is her mother dead set on her marrying Jack but the will clearly indicates that her father wished her to do so. Octavius sees all this as proof that Ann is the dutiful, self-sacrificing daughter who will marry a man she does not love. Ann feels a faint impulse of pity for this young romantic, and she does her best to let him down gently. Thus she points out that he would always worship the ground she walked on and she could never live up to his idea of divinity. He would not become disillusioned if she married Jack; so he must remain a sentimental bachelor with his romantic dreams for her sake. Tavy vows that he will kill himself, but Ann tells him that such an act would be unkind. She concedes that Jack has no illusions about her but is sure that, sometimes at least, she will enchant him. No, Tavy must not tell Jack that she wants to marry him; he would run away again. Tavy is shocked. Would Ann marry an unwilling man, he asks incredulously? He is told that there is no such thing as an unwilling man when the woman really goes after him: "The only really simple thing is to go straight for what you want and grab it." Her advice to Tavy is to keep away from women and to be content to dream about them. Still with the best intentions, Ann continues to school Tavy in the subject of women. Violet, she says, is "hard as nails," but she has great respect for the woman who is practical and who gets her own way and does so without making people sentimental about her. Tavy passionately insists that he could never marry a designing woman — not after knowing and loving Ann. Poetic to the last, he admits defeat if not comprehension. Ann pats his cheek as she says goodbye and runs into the villa.

Mrs. Whitefield enters and runs to the weeping Tavy. She learns that, following her mother's wishes, Ann intends to marry Jack. Mrs. Whitefield endeavors to enlighten him, but he cannot believe that Ann would be guilty of deceit. Tanner enters, announces that he had left the two brigands, Mendoza and Malone, together, and then asks Tavy what is the matter. Tavy sadly asks Mrs. Whitefield to tell Jack what she wishes and then leaves. Jack is puzzled, and the mother comments on how all life seems to have become so complicated. "Nothing has been right since that speech Professor Tyndale made at Belfast." (The reference is to Tyndale's famous address before the British Association for the Advancement in Science which was delivered in the early 1870's and in which the physicist declared that there was no reason to believe that mind was separate from matter.) Jack agrees that life has indeed become involved, and asks what he can do for her. She states that, whatever her wishes may be, Jack will certainly marry Ann, but he is not to blame the mother. Tanner emphatically replies that he has no intention of marrying Ann. Mrs. Whitefield expresses her hope that the two will marry, for she would like to see her daughter meet her match. Jack knows Ann for what she is, and Jack demonstrates his knowledge by describing Ann as an unscrupulous liar, a coquette, one who bullies women, and a hypocrite. He could stand everything except her "confounded hypocrisy." Mrs. Whitefield readily agrees with him and explains that, fond as she is of Tavy, she does not wish to see him suffer, whereas Jack would take care of himself very well. She adds that he must not think that she does not love Ann, her own flesh and blood, merely because she sees her daughter's faults.

Both Ann and Violet enter, the former saying that she had heard the entire conversation. Violet has come to say her farewells. She tells Jack that the sooner he gets married too, the better. Aware that the trap is closing in on him, he restively remarks that he will probably end up a married man before the day is over. Mrs. Whitefield, in tears at the thought of Violet's departure, accompanies the bride off-stage.

Ann is now alone with Tanner once more. Jack bewails the fact that everyone, even Ramsden, now treats him as if his marriage to Ann were a settled matter. Ann placidly remarks that she had not proposed to him and that he need not be married if he did not want to be. But Jack sees himself as a condemned man who has no control over his fate. He explosively denounces marriage as an "apostasy, profanation of my soul, shameful surrender, ignominious capitulation, acceptance of defeat." The sparring match between the two continues in lively fashion as Ann woos the reluctant Tanner, now without dissimulation. From their childhood, she argues, the Life Force had prepared a trap for them. Still Jack protests that he will not marry her. "Oh, you will, you will," she replies. At last he seizes her in his arms, declaring that he does love her and the Life Force enchants him. When he makes one last effort to escape her embrace, she swoons.

Most of the other characters return to the stage — Violet, Octavius, Mrs. Whitefield, Malone, Ramsden, Mendoza, and Straker. All are concerned for the well-being of Ann, who revives sufficiently to announce that Jack has promised to marry her. When Tavy bravely congratulates his friend, Jack tells him that he had not proposed but had been trapped. Ann is relieved when Violet tells her that Jack had said nothing. She appears to faint again but recovers to say that she is now quite happy. Malone is quite impressed with Jack, whom he sees as "a rough wooer," the best sort. All congratulate Jack on his happiness. But in his last speech of any length he describes his status. He is not a happy man. Both he and Ann have knowingly renounced happiness, freedom, tranquility, and especially "the romantic possibilities of an unknown future." The wedding will be the simplest possible. It will take place three days after their return to England, and it will be in the office of the district superintendent registrar. Violet calls Jack a brute, but Ann looks at him with fond pride and caresses his arm. "Go on talking," she says. "Talking!" exclaims Jack, and universal laughter bursts forth as the play ends.

SHAW'S METHOD AND TECHNIQUE

Of *Man and Superman* Shaw himself said that he had written "a trumpery story of modern London life, a life in which...the ordinary man's main business is to get means to keep up the position and habit of a gentleman and the ordinary woman's business is to get married." This suggests that the play is a comedy of manners replete with farcical elements, a play which represents no real break in the tradition of the Victorian theater. Indeed the dramatist insisted early and late that he was not an inventor in dramatic technique. In the play are to be found such familiar romantic and melodramatic elements as a will, a love triangle, the apparently fallen woman, and an episode involving capture by brigands. Among the long-lived comic types are the mother bent on marrying off her daughter; the brash, impertinent servant who knows more than his master; and such caricatures as that of Malone, the American millionnaire. In character portrayal he almost always depends upon overstatement; and such exaggeration is strictly in the tradition of the comic writer and satirist.

Like many earlier dramatists, including Shakespeare, to say nothing of Shaw's Victorian predecessors and contemporaries, the dramatist develops situations by means of a series of misunderstandings, which may be called "mistaken awarenesses." Thus he is able to build up in each successive act a series of amusing, often exciting climaxes. Early in Act I, for example, the audience witnesses a Ramsden confident that he is the sole guardian of Ann Whitefield and determined to see to it that the revolutionist Jack Tanner shall not come near her. Then, when Jack appears, Ramsden learns that, very much against his will, the younger man is to serve as co-guardian of the young lady. Dramatic irony of this sort is always satisfying to an audience. In the same act the Violet Robinson-Hector Malone subplot gets underway and begins to provide counterpoint to the main action. Like the main plot, it develops the sex theme and reveals woman as the dominant partner in the love game. Before her appearance all believe that Violet has disgraced herself. Here Shaw develops and sustains one of the finest examples of dramatic irony in modern drama. The counter-discovery, that is, the correction of mistaken awareness, is expertly handled: Violet is revealed as a respectable married woman. These situations lend themselves wonderfully to the development of character. Jack is given the opportunity to voice his advanced ideas, particularly in contrast to Ramsden, the old-fashioned liberal, when he protests against his new and unsolicited responsibility, and more particularly when he eloquently defends Violet, only to be excoriated by the young lady. Nor is all this irrelevant to the main theme, for it shows both Ann and Violet as young women who, each in her own way, are determined to get their own ways.

As the play progresses, Shaw continues to make effective use of dramatic irony. The initial dialogue between Jack Tanner and Straker lets the audience know that the blissfully ignorant Tanner is the one marked down as Ann's prey, not young Octavius. Ann enters, unaware that Jack has received Rhoda's note giving the true reason why the younger sister cannot join Tanner on the motor trip, and is caught in a lie—first-hand proof that she is absolutely unscrupulous in her pursuit of the male. Enter Hector Malone. All but Violet are unaware of the fact that he is her husband; and once more Shaw realizes the comic possibilities of the situation, which nicely balances the earlier one involving Violet. Jack volubly defends Hector and earns only the American's indignation.

In Act III, Shaw introduces a story element as melodramatic as any to be found in the Victorian theater. Not only are the protagonist and his chauffeur made captive by brigands in the Spanish Sierra, but it is revealed that Mendoza, the brigand leader, had been driven to a life of crime because of unrequited love for a young lady. Coincidence of coincidences, she turns out to be Louisa Straker, the chauffeur's sister.

Coincidence and mistaken awareness are to be found even in the Don Juan in Hell interlude. The old crone who makes inquiry to the first soul she meets turns out to be Dona Ana and learns that she is speaking to her one time lover and "murderer" of her father.

In Act IV, Malone receives and reads the note Violet had intended for Hector. This is none other than a variation of the eavesdropping device so common in the popular theater, certainly from Shakespeare's day forward. Mistaken awareness abounds in this act. Malone believes that his son is pursuing a married woman and then learns that Hector is Violet's husband. One may note how this episode also balances the one in the first act. In the main plot, it is Ann's final rejection of Octavius and Jack's realization that he cannot escape her which provide the best examples of mistaken awarenesses and subsequent discoveries.

But if *Man and Superman* is "a repertory of old state devices," to use Mr. Reuben A. Brower's term, it is also much more. For one thing, Shaw is a master of inversion. In his play the Victorian Womanly Woman as heroine is replaced by the Vital Woman who relentlessly tracks down her man. He was honest and modest enough to point out that he had not invented the pursuing female in literature: Shakespeare and many others had anticipated him in drama, and the passionate pursuing female flourished in non-dramatic narrative of the Ovidian tradition. But as far as nineteenth century and particularly Victorian drama was concerned, Shaw was an innovator. If Barrie did anticipate him in depicting a servant who was more knowledgeable than his master, Shaw nevertheless, in the character of Henry Straker, made adroit use of just such an inversion. Comic inversion is again illustrated in the characterization of Mrs. Whitefield. Many a mother in popular drama had been intent on marrying off her daughter, but where else is one to be found with the same motive for such intention? Mrs. Whitefield was devoted to Octavius as if he were a favorite son; one would expect her to welcome him as a son-in-law. But no, Tavy was too nice a boy to be victimized by Ann, whereas Jack would be a match for her. There are good examples of Shavian inversions in the Don Juan in Hell interlude also. Hell is the place where one does nothing but enjoy himself; Heaven is a boring place; Hell is the home of the Seven Deadly Virtues in whose names most of the world's misery has been caused.

The Devil, a would-be gentleman and democrat, is the one who lauds love and beauty and who wants everyone to be happy. Don Juan is anything but a condemned sensualist and murderer; he is a high-minded idealist dedicated to pure reason.

It certainly is not to be assumed that *Man and Superman* is only a composite of comic reversals, farcical incidents, and melodrama often involving type characters. As Shaw himself wrote in the dedicatory epistle, "This pleasantry is not the essence of the play." It remains a comedy *and* a philosophy. Yet one can understand why from the first performance, the play has been hailed even by those who have not the slighest interest in or knowledge of the philosophy. It happens to be good theater. And if it is filled with talk, talk, and more talk, the talk is dramatic, especially in the sense that it individualizes and develops the many characters.

Shaw is adept at varying the style of speaking from one character to another. The contrasting "voices" in the play go far to explain Harley Granville-Barker's instructions to the cast he was putting through rehearsal: "Do remember, ladies and gentlemen, that this is Italian opera." One may add to this Shaw's own remark: "My sort of play would be impossible unless I endowed my characters with powers of self-expression which they would not possess in real life." His success in individualizing the oral style of his characters may be illustrated by comparing the speeches of Ramsden and Tanner. The outmoded Ramsden does talk like "a president of highly respectable men, a chairman among directors, an alderman among counsellors, a mayor among alderman." Except when scandalized by Tanner's brash remarks, he sounds like the dignified member of Parliament used to success through the "withdrawal of opposition and the concession of comfort and precedence and power." In contrast Jack's style is more like that of the public park and street corner orator. It has an exciting, intense quality appropriate to the man who prided himself on being an iconoclast and has learned, as Shaw did, that the way to attract attention is to startle or to shock people. And it is Tanner who is master of the many sallies, jests, epigrams, and aphorisms in the play. He does not hesitate to call Ramsden an old man with obsolete ideas" and Ann "a boa constrictor," or to declare that "morality can go to its father, the Devil." To Octavius, whose own discourse offers such a marked contrast, he comes out with "perfectly revolting things sometimes." But they do not revolt the audience — quite the contrary.

Violet, who knows and has gotten exactly what she wants, namely, a rich husband, speaks far differently from Ann White- field. She minces no words; she is always direct, to the point. To the crushed Jack Tanner who had rushed to her defense, she says tersely: "I hope you will be more careful in the future of things you say." And to Hector she offers this practical counsel: "You can be as romantic as you please about love, Hector; but you must not be romantic about money." Ann, the Vital Woman and Violet's intellectual superior, can and does speak lines completely appropri- ate to one posing as the weak, helpless, and completely dutiful daughter. She easily hoodwinks Granny Ramsden and has led Octavius to believe that she is the ideal Womanly Woman. When Tanner gloomily admits that he must serve as one of her guardians, she gushes delightedly: "Then we are all agreed; and my dear father's will is to be carried out. You don't know what a joy that is to me and my mother!" But alone with Jack and aware that he sees right through her, her style of discourse changes. She is his match in the wit's combat.

Man and Superman is operatic in another way. The longer speeches, notably those made by Jack Tanner, are bravura pieces, comparable to the arias in grand opera. Examples include Tanner's conceding that he cannot wholly conquer shame, his description of the true artist when he endeavors to enlighten the love-sick Octavius, his defense of Violet, his denunication of the tyranny of mothers and of the institution of marriage. Don Juan's memorable peroration when he announces his intention of leaving Hell and going to Heaven provides another good example.

CHARACTERS

Shaw was determined to see to it that his plays were not only acted but read. Therefore he provided not only fulsome descriptions of setting and detailed stage directions but also full-length portraits of his characters. His contemporary and friend, Sir James Matthew Barrie, did much the same thing. As far as character portrayal is concerned, both were following a tradition that goes back to Ben Jonson, who was no less concerned that his plays be made available to a wide reading public. It must be conceded that, not infrequently, a given character as he is revealed in the play proper is not quite the same as he is described in the separate character sketch.

Jack Tanner

Shaw describes Tanner as "a big man with a beard, a young man of "Olympian majesty more like Jupiter than Apollo." And in the Epistle Dedicatory the dramatist castigates other writers for announcing that their heroes are geniuses and then seldom giving evidence of the fact. He therefore provided as an appendix to his play Tanner's *Revolutionist's Handbook* to prove that his hero was a great prophet, far in advance of ordinary mortals. But in the play, Tanner is not heroic, nor is he a genius in the sense that he translates ideas into actions. He talks, according to Mr. Eric Bentley. Shaw gave him the appearance of H. M. Hyndman, founder of the Democratic Federation in 1885 and for a time the leader of English Socialism—the man with whom Shaw came to differ as regards Marxist economic determinism. At one level, then, Shaw was satirizing the parlor socialist who was as voluble and inflammatory as Jack Tanner, but who never turned words into actions. As a matter of fact, Shaw was perfectly capable of satirizing Fabianism, especially in view of the fact that, for the nonce, he had lost faith in a political solution to a man's problems.

But when Harley Granville-Barker created the stage role of Jack Tanner he made himself up to look as much like Shaw as possible. There is indeed much of Shaw in the hero's character. In one of his weekly articles (quoted by Mr. Bentley) Shaw wrote: "It is instinct with me personally to attack every idea which has been full grown ten years." This is exactly what Tanner does. He does not hesitate to call Ramsden an old fuddy-duddy to Ramsden's face and to advise him to cultivate a little impudence and to welcome heterodox opinions. Tanner himself does both—witness his tirades against the tyranny of greybeards and of mothers, his redefining of morality in terms shocking to the conventional. Shaw uses Tanner to purify the intellectual air. It is he who seeks to clarify the relationship between the sexes, to debunk what Shaw considered Victorian smugness and hypocrisy, to ridicule the romanticism of the Tavies and (more important) to expound his latest theory relating to the advance of the race through eugenics. Thus Tanner is intended to represent what Shaw believed to be the true moral sense. This is clearly revealed in the first long dialogue between Jack and Ann in Act I. Jack had acknowledged the fact that he had been destructive as a boy but insisted that he is now ten times as destructive, for his destructiveness is directed toward moral ends.

So Jack Tanner, by means of his own testimony, is identified as High Priest of Vitalism and Life Force. Nevertheless he does nothing but talk. Before Ann's relentless attack, Jack retreats almost in panic—and finally concedes her the victory. But to do justice to him, one must remember that he scintillates, whether he is bewailing his fate as Ann's co-guardian, amusingly discussing his chauffeur as the New Man, exchanging courtesies with the brigand leader who has made him captive, comically denouncing Ann as a boa constrictor and a tigress, or voicing his utter terror at the thought of marriage. It is significant that Jack holds the friendship of the idealistic Octavius and that not even Ramsden protests when his engagement to Ann is announced.

Ann Whitefield

Shaw wrote to Lillian MacCarthy, for whom he created the role of Ann Whitefield: "Don't have any blue ribbon and muslin: use violet or purple...There should be a certain pomegranate splendour lurking in the effect." And in the stage directions he calls her "one of the vital geniuses," adding that she is not oversexed, which would be a "vital defect, not a true excess." Although Shaw also states that whether or not she is good-looking depends upon individual taste, in different ways she fascinates such different individuals as Ramsden, Octavius, and Tanner.

To the gullible Ramsden, whom with the suggestion of both genuine affection and slight contempt she calls "Granny," she is "a wonderfully dutiful girl." He is unable to remember any time when she expressed her own wishes as a reason for doing something or not doing it. She would always say, "Father wished me to" or "Mother wouldn't like it." It has, apparently, always been her self-lessness and her keen sense of duty which have motivated her conduct. Even in childhood she had broken up the experimental love affair between Jack Tanner and "a girl named Rachael Rosetree" because she felt it was her duty to do so. This is the role she plays so successfully for the Ramsdens and Tavies of the world. She is full of sweet sentiments; she is daintily coy and appealingly help-less; she even swoons in the presence of young men as is expected of the feminine, well-bred young Victorian Womanly Woman.

Octavius the innocent is easily deceived by her. When Jack, trying to enlighten him, vehemently exclaims: "Vitality in a woman is a blind fury of creation. She sacrifices herself to it: do you think she will hesitate to sacrifice you?" Tavy rushes to the defense of his goddess. "Why it is just because she is self-sacrificing that she will not sacrifice those she loves." He remains incredulous when Jack tells him that it "is the self-sacrificing woman that sacrifices others most recklessly."

If Ann is to Octavius the "reality of romance" she is nothing of the kind to her mother or certainly to Jack Tanner. In the stage directions Shaw sums up an important aspect of her character in these words: "She inspires confidence as a person who will do nothing she does not mean to do; also some fear, perhaps, as a woman will probably do everything she means to do without taking more account of other people than may be necessary and what she calls right. In short, what the weaker of her own sex sometimes call a cat." Her analysis of Violet is a frank tribute of one expert on getting what she wants to another expert who uses a different technique. To Octavius, whom she is trying to let down easily, she says: "You are soft-hearted! It's queer that you should be so different from Violet. Violet's hard as nails." When Octavius protests that his sister is "thoroughly womanly at heart," Ann replies with some impatience: "Why do you say that? Is it unwomanly to be thoughtful and business-like and sensible? Do you want Violet to be an idiot—or something worse like me?" She concludes that she has great respect for Violet because Violet always gets her way.

It is the Ann who always intends to get her way who nearly terrifies Jack Tanner. The latter describes her as a liar, a bully, a hypocrite — as one who is utterly unscrupulous in using her personal fascination to make men give her what she wants. To him, she is "something for which there is no polite name." In the course of the play one does see her "bully" people into doing what she wants; one does hear her tell lies — and being caught in a big one. She is indeed depicted in bold strokes. One can understand why Mr. Eric Bentley sees her as a black widow spider out to trap the male, use him for her purposes, and then devour him. She is anything but the thoroughly *average* woman at heart, and her methods are more virile than feminine.

Of course Shaw was a man with a thesis and a program in this comedy which is also a philosophy. Ann is the archetype of the Vital Woman. If Jack preaches vitality, it is Ann who practices it. Unlike Violet, she has no need to seek out a rich husband; she is already well-to-do. The great mission in her life is to find the right father for her children. Driven by instinct, she knows herself to be the instrument towards creating the superior race of the future. In the last analysis, nothing else matters to her. So, fascinating as even her severest critic, Jack Tanner, finds her to be, she is a kind of female Machiavellian, using any and all means to fulfill her destiny.

Ann Whitefield plays her role beautifully so that one can understand why most of the other characters in the play are deceived by her. Apparently her delicate sensibilities have been cruelly shocked by her mother's crass reference to Mr. Whitefield's death, and she hastily leaves the room to conceal her emotions. But we know that she had been looking for an excuse to leave anyway. When Jack speaks of her unsatiable curiosity leading her to tempt boys, she is again shocked. "All timid women are conventional, Jack, or else we are so cruelly, so vilely misunderstood." So dedicated is she in her role of the Vital Woman with a mission of overwhelming importance that she has no interest in Jack's *Revolutionist's Handbook*. When he tries to explain that his goal in life is to "shatter creeds and demolish idols," she is merely bored. "I am afraid I am too feminine to see any sense in destruction." If this does not deflate him, Ann adds: "I don't mind your queer opinions one little bit."

In terms of the theory of creative evolution which informs this play, then, Ann actually is unselfish; it is the future of the race which is at stake, not the fortunes of the individual caught in present time.

Roebuck Ramsden

"Annie's Granny" is the old-fashioned liberal holding on to views advanced some thirty years ago. Among his heroes are John Bright (1811-1889), outstanding spokesman for the industrialists and opponent of the Corn Laws; and Herbert Spencer (1820-1903), English philosopher, known for his application of scientific doctrines of evolution to philosophy and ethics. Shaw describes him as a man of means living in ease and comfort, and tells us that Ramsden is "more than a respectable man: he is marked out as a president of highly respectable men." His active civil life has given him "his broad air of importance." Harmlessly vain and rather smug, he has been used to having his views prevail. His opening discourse with Octavius reveals him as the pontifical master of platitudes. It is with reason that Jack Tanner calls him Polonius, the vain Lord Chamberlain to King Claudius in *Hamlet*. Although he prides himself on his "progressive" position, he is the complete conformist. As Shaw tells us even the clothes he wears "harmonize with the religions of respectable men." He invariably holds to his moth-eaten opinions and to his favorite authors, recoiling in dismay, if not horror, when a brand new idea is introduced. Ramsden denies that Tanner's *Revolutionist's Handbook* is too advanced for him. Yet he refuses to read the copy which had been sent to him. Moreover, when his alleged liberalism is put to the test by the report concerning Violet, he fails. Clever Jack Tanner has little difficulty in forcing him to forego his "duty" and abnegate his "principles" relating to the English home. Playing up to him as the prototype of the Victorian Womanly Woman, Ann Whitefield knows just how to handle Ramsden. His shocked outbursts in response to Tanner's sweeping generalizations provide much of the fun in the first two acts of the play.

Octavius Robinson

Shaw writes that Octavius comes straight from Mozart's *Don Giovanni*. He is, to be sure, the faithful and ardent lover of Ann

Whitefield, although not engaged to her. He is further identified as the "artist man" — as a poet, to be specific. But he possesses none of the qualities which Jack Tanner enumerates when he lectures Octavius on the subject. He never could be unscrupulous or half vivisector, half vampire to women; and surely he could never be "a child-robber, a blood-sucker, a hypocrite, and a cheat whose justification for his being is that he shows us ourselves as we really are." Jack's tirade only bewilders this young romanticist.

Octavius is "really an uncommonly nice looking young fellow," and everything in his appearance announces "the man who will love and suffer later on." Ann calls him Ricky-Ticky-Tavy, half affectionately, half contemptuously. The allusion, of course, is to the pet mongoose in Kipling's well-known story. The sobriquet, therefore, is hardly flattering; yet Octavius remains a "nice young man." He is a kind of a pet to Ramsden and to Mrs. Whitefield, who likes him and his sister better than she does her own children. Like Ramsden, Octavius is completely taken in by Ann, whom he adores. And he readily believes her when she tells him that her parents wished her to marry Jack Tanner and that she must honor their wishes. His romanticism extends beyond his worship for Ann. When Hector quixotically announces that he will work for a living and no longer depend upon his rich father, Octavius is affected almost to tears. The perspicacious Ann Whitefield is exactly right: Octavius is far different from his down-to-earth, practical sister, Violet. He always has been a "really good boy," and he will always be nice to women. But as Ann predicts he will remain the sentimental bachelor holding fast to his illusions. He provides an amusing contrast to his friend, the iconoclastic Jack Tanner.

Violet Robinson

No modest violet, Octavius' attractive sister is womanly enough, but in the sense made clear by Ann Whitefield. In reply to Ann's statement that Violet is "hard as nails," Octavius insists that she is "thoroughly womanly at heart." Ann then asks: "Is it unwomanly to be thoughtful and businesslike and sensible? Do you want Violet to be an idiot — or something worse like me?" She certainly is no idiot; she is a young lady who knows exactly what she wants and who gets it. Ann admires her especially because she does so "without coaxing—without having to make people sentimental about her." She is much too practical to defy convention, thus her dislike of Jack Tanner and her expression of outrage when the well-meaning self-styled revolutionist rushes to her defense. Whereas Ann wants a father for her children and is concerned with the future of the race, Violet is interested in getting an affluent husband who will provide nourishment and creature comforts on the grand scale and who will not be so romantic as to want to work for them if he does not have to. One may be sure that she married the son of an American millionaire confident that she would be able to win over the father who is dead-set on having his son marry an aristocrat. The skill with which she does exactly that and the firmness with which she schools Hector add appreciably to the comedy. Malone, who first angrily declared that Violet had married a beggar, is soon begging her to accept a thousand dollar bill and pleading with her to bring Hector to his senses.

Mrs. Whitefield

"All timid women are conventional," says Ann to Jack Tanner at one point in the action. Mrs. Whitefield is timid and she is conventional. Shaw uses her to develop his ideas of parent-children repulsion, a theme which he had introduced into one of his novels, *Immaturity,* wherein Robert Smith is described as being revolted by the "solemn humbug" which his parents inflict upon him. Thus it is that Mrs. Whitefield complains to Tanner: "I don't know why it is that other people's children are so nice to me, and my own have so little consideration for me. It's no wonder I don't seem able to care for Ann and Rhoda as I do for Tavy and Violet." Tanner's devastating comment goes completely over her head: "I suspect that the tables of consanguinity have a natural basis of natural repugnance."

Mrs. Whitefield is the prototype of the Victorian mother and Womanly Woman. Advanced ideas, such as those expressed by Tyndale in his Belfast address, only disturb and bewilder her. Yet, as Shaw tells us in the stage directions, she has an "expression of muddled shrewdness" and a "squeak of protest in her voice." She is aware that she is looked upon as being spineless and ineffectual. But her shrewdness, however muddled, makes it possible for her to see that her daughter is predatory; and the "squeak of protest" is translated into action of sorts since she ardently hopes that Jack, who sees through Ann also, will marry Ann. After all, Tavy is too nice a boy to be made to suffer as Ann's husband.

Henry Straker

Since Shaw had introduced the New Woman into British drama, it is not surprising that he did the same thing for the New Man. Enry Straker is the characteristic phenomenon of the New Age; he is the efficient mechanic, the product of the new technological education which ultimately will eliminate the ordinary working man. In the Dedicatory Epistle, Shaw stated that Straker is "an intentional dramatic sketch for the contemporary of Mr. H. G. Wells's anticipation of the efficient engineering class which will, he hopes, sweep the jabberers out of the way of civilization." In view of the fact that Jack Tanner is pre-eminently one of the "jabberers," Enry's role as Tanner's remarkable chauffeur is quite amusing.

Though no ordinary workman, Straker is aware that he is one of the indispensable men. Tanner wryly remarks: "I am slave to that car and you." Later, Violet explains to Malone: "I am sorry, Mr. Malone, if that man has been rude to you. But what can we do? He is our chauffeur...we are dependent upon him." Whether or not he believes that his schools are better than the universities as Tanner insists, Enry remains satisfied with his own training. And if he speaks cockney English, it is with the confidence that English so should be spoken. When Malone corrects him, he replies with calm superiority: "Hector in your own country; thats what comes o livin in provincial places like Ireland and America. Over here your Ector: if you aint noticed it before, you soon will."

Yet Enry is tolerant enough. When Tanner says, "You despise Oxford, Enry, don't you?" the chauffeur replies: "No I don't. Very nice sort of place. They teach you to be a gentleman there. In the Polytechnic they teach you to be an engineer or such like. See?" He is not devoid of culture, despite the fact that Tanner accuses him of being a Philistine. He sets Tanner right when the latter attributes to Voltaire a saying that Enry knows is to be found in "Bow Mar Shay."

Finally, Enry is something of a realist. When Octavius virtuously states that he believes in the dignity of labor, the chauffeur dryly replies: "That's because you've never done any, Mr. Robinson." Again in reply to Tanner's statement that he is "a bit of a Socialist" himself, Enry remarks: "Most rich men are, I notice." And, of course, he knows more about women than does his master. It is he who first alerts Jack Tanner to the fact that Tanner is Ann's intended victim.

Hector Malone, Jr.

In the words of Mr. Arthur H. Nethercot (*Men and Supermen,* 1954), Hector is Shaw's Manly Man. And Shaw has no more respect for him than he has for the Womanly Woman; he is an object of satire. On the credit side Shaw tells us that he has an "engaging freshness of...personality," that he is chivalrous to women, and that his "vein of easy humour" is "rather amusing when it ceases to puzzle" his audience. But he is the ultra-romantic, and it is this quality which makes him so attractive and admirable to Octavius. He is almost oppressively moral and noble; his standards are those of the strict Puritan. As Shaw puts it, "English life seems to him to suffer from a lack of edifying rhetoric (which he calls moral tone); English behavior to shew a want of respect for womanhood...: English society to be plain spoken to an extent which stretches occasionally to intolerable coarseness..." Add to this the fact that he dislikes politics and is intellectually bankrupt and a rather ridiculous figure emerges.

Hector is nothing if not noble. He is shocked to the marrow of his moral being to learn that his father had read a letter intended for the son, although Violet reasonably points out that the error was completely understandable. He denounces his father and, mouthing high sounding terms, declares that he will not take a penny more from him—that as of that afternoon he has become a Working Man. One can join Tanner in exclaiming: "No wonder American women prefer to live in Europe."

Hector Malone, Sr.

Malone is even more of a caricature than his son, depicted as he is as a robber-baron in the capitalistic world. It is the Fabian

Shaw who comes to the fore in the dramatic characterization here. In his first reported public speech delivered in January, 1885, before the Industrial Remuneration Society, Shaw grouped the capitalist speculator with the burglar and the gouging landlord: "all three inflict on community an injury of precisely the same nature."

Malone is described in anything but complimentary terms. He is a man who is "vulgar in his finery"; a "bullet cheeked man with a red complexion, stubby hair, smallish eyes, a hard mouth that folds down at the corners, and a dogged chin"; "he has the self-confidence of one who has made money, and something of the truculence of one who has made it in a brutalizing struggle." In the play his materialism is specifically shown by his insistence that his son's marriage must "show social profit somewhere." He is the largest shareholder in Mendoza, Ltd., the brigand's enterprise. Understandably, Tanner, himself a benefactor under the capitalistic system and one who cheerfully remarked that he lived by robbing the poor, knows that these two will get along famously.

But Violet calls Malone a romantic, and has little difficulty in winning him over to her point of view. In the sense that, as Shaw believed, an individual's frantic pursuit of money and more money is the evasion of true reality, Malone is indeed a romanticist. His obsession that his son marry someone "with a handle to her name" is a manifestation of this form of romanticism.

Mendoza

The brigand-poetaster is depicted as a rather attractive man in his way. He is tall and strong; he has a fine speaking voice and a ready wit. His manners, one may reasonably assume, he learned as a waiter. "Hence my cosmopolitanism," he explained in reference to his former occupation. Inevitably he became the organizer and leader of his group, and he presides with dignity and skill at the evening meetings of the Socialist debating society high in the Spanish Sierra. If he is a man with "a Mephistophelean affectation," a swagger, and a certain sentimentality, his pre-eminence is unquestioned.

54

Mendoza greets Tanner in the correct manner; he is the soul of decorum. He brushes aside thoughts of discussing the ransom immediately: business can wait while he plays the solicitous host. He is, to be sure, a romanticist. Unrequited love for Louisa Straker, cook in a private home, had driven him to banditry. Consistent with his romanticism, he is an unrestrained writer and reciter of love poetry.

Unsuccessful in love as he has been, Mendoza has nevertheless found his true calling—the robbing of the rich in order, as he explains, to correct the "injustice of the existing distribution of wealth." He has proved his capabilities by getting Malone to invest in his enterprise, although the American millionaire knew none of the details concerning it at the time of his investment.

Don Juan Tenorio

Jack Tanner's aristocratic ancestor does indeed resemble Tanner but is not to be confused with his still earth-bound descendant. Shaw describes him as having "a more critical, fastidious, handsome face, paler and colder, without Tanner's impetuous credulity and enthusiasm, and without a touch of his plutocratic vulgarity." His manners are impeccable. Although he expresses his beliefs with conviction, he does not depend upon shocking his listeners as Jack does. He is the archetype of the philosophic man whom he honors in his long autobiographical speech. He tells in detail how he had developed intellectually. From the Artist, romantic man, he had learned to worship woman; from her he learned the truth about the relationship between the sexes and the roles of the male and the female in the larger scheme of Nature. Thus he was led to the higher truth relating to man's destiny.

It is Don Juan who explains to Dona Ana that all wicked people are comfortable in Hell and that Hell is "the home of the unreal and of the seekers of happiness," as well as the "home of honor, duty, justice, and the rest of the seven deadly virtues," in whose name all the evil in the world is done. He himself long since has rejected comfort and happiness as man's goal in life. Moreover, he had "repudiated all duty, trampled honor underfoot, and laughed at justice." In a word, he is not one of the wicked, and he does not feel comfortable in Hell; the place bores him insufferably. The Devil describes him as a "cold, selfish egotist." But Don Juan is not disturbed by this satanic estimate of his character. He is nauseated by the Devil's sentimentality and smugness, and especially by the Devil's smooth rationalization of his beliefs and activities.

Don Juan is the accomplished platform lecturer. Along with *The Revolutionist's Handbook* his speeches embody the dominant ideas in the play. Chief among these is the mystical creed of Life Force. It is Don Juan who first introduces this term. His ambition is to spend the rest of his days in profound contemplation which will lead, he is sure, to the ultimate emergence of Philosophical Man—Superman of the future. Inevitably, then, he renounces Hell, the abode of self-deceivers, and leaves for Heaven, the abode of the true Realists.

Dona Ana De Ulloa

This is Ann Whitefield some 300 years earlier and before the emergence of the pursuing woman. A faithful Catholic who had never failed to go to confession, she is appalled to find herself in hell. She is no less shocked to learn that her father, who had been translated to Heaven, is on the best of terms with the Devil. The fact of the matter is, as Don Juan explains, that she is still one "of the unreal and of the seekers of happiness." When the earthly Don Juan had proclaimed his love for her, she had screamed as a matter of duty, and the fatal duel had ensued. Thus motivated by one of the seven deadly virtues, she was really responsible for evil. For a time she remains incredulous that she should be in the realm of the damned: "I, who sacrificed all my inclinations to womanly virtue and propriety!"

Dona Ana particularly resents Don Juan's concept of a woman's mind and his conviction that marriage is "the most licentious of human institutions" and "a mantrap baited with simulated accomplishments and delusive idealizations." All this is to her "cynical and disgusting materialism," and she vies with Don Juan himself in vehemence as she defends the institution of marriage as viewed by the proper, conventional young lady.

Changed from an old crone into a lady of twenty-seven Dona Ana has all the grace and attractiveness of Ann Whitefield. She is not convinced by the arguments made by the Devil and supported by the Statue. At the last she is deeply moved by Don Juan's idealism and eloquence, and by his determination to leave Hell and spend his days in Heaven, "the home of the masters of reality." Once she grasps the idea of Life Force and of the Superman, she is not swerved by the Devil's remark that Superman does not yet exist and probably never will. Fervently she exclaims: "Not yet created! Then my work is not yet done...A father! a father for the superman."

Audiences have remained uncertain whether or not Dona Ana was "apotheosized" — that is, followed Don Juan to Heaven, thus assuming the role of the Vital Woman in pursuit of the superior male. The Devil assures her that she will be in his palace before he and the Statue get there. Shaw himself, in an explanatory note, part of his summary of the Don Juan in Hell interlude, wrote: "Love is neither her pleasure nor her study: it is her business. So she, in the end, neither goes with Don Juan to heaven nor with the devil and her father to the palace of pleasure, but declares that her work is not yet finished. For though by her death she is done with the bearing of men to mortal fathers, she may yet, a Woman Immortal, bear the Superman to the Eternal Father."

The Devil

His Satanic Majesty, who rules in his palace of pleasure, is "not at all unlike Mendoza," although much older. His manners would seem to be perfect, but it is apparent that they are a veneer put on by one who is actually rather vulgar. When one recalls that Mendoza, the waiter turned brigand, was an incurable romantic suffering from unrequited love for a cook, and that he was a poet of sorts, one can understand why, among all the characters in the play proper, the Devil should resemble him. Certainly Shaw's Devil is no more terrifying than Mendoza and quite as accomplished as a speaker. Moreover, he is the thoroughgoing democrat, for he knows that the majority of mankind, particularly in England, are dreamers and drifters like him. He is content to leave Heaven to those few who recognize and accept reality and who are not pleasure seekers. Nevertheless, he is vain enough to resent the fact that Don Juan leaves Hell: this is a political defeat for the Devil.

The Devil is a master at self-exculpation, constantly feeling that he must explain and justify himself. Despite a kind of affability which seems to emanate from him, he becomes "peevish and sensitive when his advances are not reciprocated." He is quite voluble in denouncing those who (like Milton in *Paradise Lost*) have "misrepresented" him. On occasion he can mouth witty and startling aphorisms worthy of a Jack Tanner, as when he declares, "An Englishman thinks he is moral when he is only uncomfortable." And his devastating indictment of man as a destructive creature, in which he sums up the crimes of the past century and predicts more terrible ones to come, is worthy of a Jonathan Swift. But he is not a thinker; he is notoriously shallow, and his wit is usually forced or feeble. Unlike Don Juan, who is no less aware of man's pretentions and failures, he is content to drift. His solution is for man to seek haven in an illusory world where he can luxuriate in the tender emotions and not disturb himself about serious moral, political, and economic problems. Let man merely *imagine* that he is living—that is the Devil's advice. So his Hell, so attractive to the Statue and to most others, is the realm of the sentimentalists who talk eternally of love and beauty; it is a realm where everyone is comfortable, not having to exert themselves intellectually on the behalf of mankind.

The Statue

The Commander of Calatrava, who has chosen to retain his sculptured form because it is more flattering to him than was his fleshly form, suggests Ramsden. But the Statue hardly views himself as an advanced thinker. Indeed, as he says, he is happy not to have to think at all: "I'm quite content with brains enough to know that I am enjoying myself. Why should I want to understand it?... My experience is that one's pleasures don't bear thinking about." Harmlessly vain, he insists that Don Juan bested him in the duel only because his foot had slipped; and Don Juan plays up to his vanity, cheerfully acknowledging his superiority as a duelist. He still prides himself upon having been a valiant soldier and is almost provoked into another duel when Don Juan scoffingly refers to "that vulgar pageant of incompetent schoolboyish gladiators which you call the Army" and then adds that "When the military man approaches, the world locks up its spoons and packs off its womanhood."

Determined to embrace unreality and live content in Hell, the Statue nevertheless is quite honest about himself and acknowledges the validity of many statements made by Don Juan. Excusing himself to the shocked Dona Ana, saying that Don Juan "has stripped every rag of decency from the discussion," he says that he "may as well tell the frozen truth." He then admits that Don Juan's argument that woman is the pursuer in the love game is sound and that he had often lied when making love to women.

It is the Statue who tells Don Juan that there are no beautiful women or artists in Heaven — intelligence which makes the Spaniard all the more anxious to go there. And he is impressed by Don Juan's conception of the Superman. The Devil is impelled to caution him against "these Life Worshippers": "Do not listen to their gospel, Senor Commander: it is dangerous. Beware of the pursuit of the Superhuman: it leads to an indiscriminate contempt for Heaven." So the pleasure-loving Statue leaves with the Devil through a trap door.

CAESAR AND CLEOPATRA NOTES

THE PROLOGUE

In the dark, gloomy Temple of Ra, Ra himself (an Egyptian sun god) appears; he stands in the central doorway, mysteriously lighted. His hawk's head surveys the audience contemptuously, and he silences the audience's chatter with a single word: "Peace!" His command is ironic, for it is no benediction. He is demanding silence from these "quaint little islanders." He is about to explain to them the nature of the play which they are about to see. Clearly, he doubts their ability to fathom its content or its personages, yet he continues.

Sarcastically, he surveys the men before him and sums them up as simpletons "with white paper on [their] chests and nothing written thereon"; he refers to the women in the audience as cunning hypocrites who "alluringly...conceal [their] thoughts" about their husbands. Collectively, he sees the audience as mindless sheep—fools, like all the "other fools" who have lived in the interim between Caesar's time and theirs. Yet in Caesar's time, the Egyptians erected pyramids which still stand; the "dust-heaps" which this audience calls "empires" will "scatter in the wind."

Still, however, he hopes that the audience will see at least one parallel between the time of this drama and their own time. Then, the Romans "stood between the old Rome and the new." Today's generation of English people stands between "an old England and a new." Then, as now, the populace and its people were "perplexed." Didactically, Ra points out that old Rome was characterized by its greatness because its greatness was characterized by its simple nature "...and the gods pitied it and helped it and strengthened it and shielded it." The new Rome characterized itself by its greed; it robbed its own poor, then it robbed the poor of other nations, and eventually it became rich and huge, and its dominion spread over the earth.

In this time between the old Rome and the new Rome, two mighty Romans emerged—Pompey the Great and Julius Caesar. The gods favored

Caesar because he valued wit, and he ruled because he was a great talker and a politician; eventually, in his middle age, he changed; he became a warrior and was successful because people acquiesced to him ("such is the nature of you mortals"). In contrast, Pompey was no thinker; he was only a warrior — nothing more. Therefore, he was not a favorite of the gods, and they spitefully allowed him to rise to the pinnacle of power before they destroyed him "so that his fall might be the more terrible."

The Egyptians helped the gods destroy Pompey. They looked on as Caesar and Pompey, these two mighty dog-eat-dog warriors battled for supremacy on Egyptian soil; then the Egyptians cleverly asked Lucius Septimius, a soldier of Pompey's, to murder his general. He did so; he beheaded the mighty "dog" and presented Pompey's head like a "pickled cabbage" to Caesar. Thus ended the battle for Egypt.

Ra speaks of the other element in this drama which they will presently see: Cleopatra, "an unchaste woman," yet only "a child...whipped by her nurse...a child queen" when the middle-aged Caesar became enamored of her.

Once again, Ra surveys the audience before him; he sees only "dull folk," folk as dull as all those who have lived since the days of Caesar and Cleopatra. He counsels these dullards to listen to Caesar, for Caesar was a wise man and also a great man — "as ye count greatness," he adds sardonically. He himself will not speak again; he requests no applause.

Clearly, Ra is Shaw's mouthpiece; Shaw is paralleling the Roman occupation of Egypt with England's occupation of Morocco, in addition to England's occupation of its other "colonial dominions." For two thousand years after Caesar's time, men continue to battle for dominance of land. "War is a wolf," Ra says; it is a wolf that will eventually "come to your own door." The play that the audience is about to see will concern a warrior's martial values; it will also concern his passions. Shaw hoped that his dramas would teach; every one of his plays has a central "message"; like Ra, Shaw believed that most of his audience lacked the minds to think deeply about what they were seeing and they likewise lacked the courage to grow and mature. Like Ra, Shaw continued talking; occasionally, he was contemptuous; usually, he was cynical. He was always serious, yet he was ever witty.

AN ALTERNATIVE TO THE PROLOGUE

Shaw offers the director an alternative to Ra's long and mannered monologue. In order to catch the interest of the audience and provide exposition, Shaw suggests opening the play with a brief scene — one that begins with casual carousing and ends in chaos. He speaks to the director very professionally about the staging, instructing him precisely about the set and about the lighting, meanwhile quipping very familiarly about things very British. For example, he suggests that Cleopatra's palace be an old Syrian building made of "whitened mud," but "not so ugly as Buckingham Palace," and he says that the Egyptian palace guards should be much like English soldiers, except that the Egyptians are "more civilized" — that is, they do not "mutilate" their enemies (he refers here to the English people's dismemberment of Cromwell's corpse). In addition, Shaw acidly characterizes each of the main characters who will be on stage when the curtain rises; Belzanor, the Egyptian general, is a brute of a warrior, who is childishly playing dice with a Persian messenger; the messenger has just brought what should be alarming news: the Romans are coming. But Belzanor is more interested in the dice game, and his first utterance is a mild oath (evoking the name of a god whom one would expect to find only in a crossword puzzle or in a footnote). Belzanor has lost the dice game to the Persian messenger, and there is no chance to retaliate, for another messenger, Bel Affris, has arrived, bringing more news about the Roman legions. Caesar's army is now only a short distance from the palace walls. Belzanor boasts that *he* is not afraid of Julius Caesar. Belzanor is "descended from the gods"; to this, the Persian wryly observes that "the gods are not always good to their poor relations."

Bel Affris tries to convince Belzanor that the Roman soldiers are unlike the Egyptian troops; the Romans "care nothing about cowardice... they fight to win...pride and honor" are nothing to them. He himself was in a legion that fell; he survived only because he stood firm. The Romans respected that virtue: "no man," he says, "attacks a lion when the field is full of sheep"; the "descendants of the gods," he continues, "fled in fear," and the "battle was not to the strong...the race was to the swift."

Bel Affris asks Belzanor what they should do to save the Egyptian women from the Romans. Belzanor suggests killing them — death before dishonor. The Persian suggests, however, that if even some survive that the Romans could demand "blood money"; hence, it would be better to let the Romans kill them: "it is cheaper." Shaw comments to the director that Belzanor should appear "awestruck" by the Persian's "brain power."

At this point, the foremost problem concerns the queen. Belzanor is ready to toss her across the rump of his horse and carry her out of Caesar's reach. Clearly, he doesn't think too highly of her, or of any woman, but whereas he is a descendant of the gods, Cleopatra is a descendant of the Nile. And if the Nile were to refuse to rise, all Egypt would perish. Thus Cleopatra must be protected.

The Persian suggests a plan: Caesar is said to be a great lover of women; yet he is too old for young women, and old women are too wise to worship him. In contrast, there is Cleopatra, a young nymphet—not quite a woman and not yet wise. Cleopatra's youth and innocence could be used to their advantage. Belzanor follows the Persian's logic, and he demands that the queen's chief nurse, Ftatateeta, bring Cleopatra to him.

Ftatateeta, old and sinewy, with "the mouth of a bloodhound and the jaws of a bulldog," enters. She mocks Belzanor's arrogant orders; he does not frighten her. As Cleopatra's nurse, she herself has some control over the Nile. She tells Belzanor that Cleopatra has been missing since dawn and suggests that perhaps he can find her "in the shadow of the Sphinx." The queen has often been carrying around the sacred cats and whispering her secrets to them; if she has learned that the Romans are coming, then perhaps she has gone to the Sphinx—especially since the sacred white cat is missing. She threatens them, however, with destruction if any harm should come to the queen.

The stage suddenly erupts with guardsmen and a mob of fugitives, and general panic ensues. Torches are thrown down and extinguished, and as the curtain falls, there is only "darkness and dead silence." One is now ready for the play itself.

In reading any play, one misses, of necessity, the prime ingredient: the drama onstage. In Shaw's plays, however, there is some recompense in reading them, for Shaw includes, along with the text, an abundance of witty asides and pungent observations. As one reads one of Shaw's plays, one is always aware of Shaw himself. Here, Shaw delights in poking fun at the British by lauding their Egyptian counterparts; yet when we actually hear and visualize these counterparts, they turn out to be absolute fools. The two characters whom we admire most in this alternative prologue turn out to be underlings. Shaw erects pedestals for his so-called heroes, then yanks them off. This Alternative Prologue is first-rate capsulated Shaw. He excels in debunking and deflating. This is the key to this prologue; Shaw is setting up in miniature exactly what he will do throughout the entirety of *Caesar and Cleopatra*. He means to examine our notions of heroism, femininity, intelligence, and morality—then turn them inside out—with style and immodest critical brilliance.

ACT I

This act contains a series of jolting revelations, all designed to demolish our preconceived notions about Caesar and about Cleopatra. The characters who emerge from the darkness that closes both of Shaw's prologues do not resemble either of the traditional fictional characters, nor any of the historical accounts of these personages, nor do they resemble any of the illustrations of them that have filled textbooks or literary classics. These characters are creations of Shaw. We are looking through Shaw's eyes, from his point of view, and he focuses on two very mortal and very flawed human beings; moreover, he places these uniquely conceived characters on a startlingly designed stage.

As the "silver mist" of the moon gradually lightens the stage, we realize that we are staring into the eyes of a gigantic Sphinx. In the past, when we have seen pictures of it, the Sphinx has usually been pictured in profile. Here, we confront this massive half-human, half-beast head on. Visually, what we see is startling; verbally, what we will be hearing will be a dramatic parallel to this stunning theatrical effect. The Sphinx dominates the stage, and when we overcome our initial awe of it, we focus on what lies between its gigantic paws; atop a "heap of red poppies" is a little girl's body; she has braided hair and is sleeping gently. This is Sweet Innocence in the arms of dark, exotic Mystery; this is Beauty and the Beast. The young girl, amidst the pool of red poppies could conceivably be a sacrifical offering to this eroding, monstrous stone god. As we gaze at this scene on the Nile, we are inundated by a flood of associations—none of which will be correct.

As we are trying to fathom this puzzling enigma on stage, we are diverted abruptly by a man's loud and arrogant voice: "Hail, Sphinx." The voice is Caesar's, and it is a Caesar who, for a moment, reassures us; we recognize this man, we think; at least he *seems* like the Caesar of history books. This is another of Shaw's dramatic tricks, for in a few moments, just when we feel comfortable with this overdrawn, bold personage, Shaw is going to expose all of Caesar's nonheroic nature. But momentarily Shaw gives us the illusion that this man is the mythic Caesar. This man postures; he is a weary Titan, alien from the human race because of his greatness. Nowhere can he find his equal. He is terribly lonely and terribly aware of his being very special, singled out for immortal honor. Because of his uniqueness, his way has never been *his* way; his way has always been "the way of destiny," and it has led him over most of the world.

This is effective nineteenth-century style melodrama: the hero, cloaked in dark night, emerges; he comes to stage center and proclaims the agony of his soul. The parody works here, and we can appreciate Shaw's wit after only a few sentences. Shaw is satirizing this hero of history; Caesar's soliloquy to the Sphinx is pompous and poetic; it is the rhetoric of an immature egomaniac. Caesar sighs that he has found no earthly equal; yet, at least, he has found the Sphinx — almost an equal. But even that thought is not ultimately comforting because Caesar realizes that while he conquers, the Sphinx endures. As a result, Caesar's agony overflows once more — until he realizes that at least he feels more at home *here* than he did in Rome, in Gaul, in Britain, in Spain, *et. al.* Thus Caesar and the Sphinx stand before us, in Caesar's words, "silent, full of thoughts, alone in the silver desert."

This tableau is broken by the shy voice of a child, calling out cautiously, "Old gentleman." Caesar has just finished boasting of his mighty, manly conquests, and now we hear this wee voice characterizing him as an "old gentleman." The juxtaposition jars us; it unnerves Caesar. At first, he assumes that the Sphinx is speaking. Such a thing *is* possible; after all, according to Caesar, he and the Sphinx are near-equals. Then he spies the little girl, cradled in the Sphinx's embrace. Repeatedly, she urges him to climb up: the Romans are coming, and they will eat him up. This is a dream. It cannot be happening, and this little girl cannot possibly be who she says she is — Cleopatra, Queen of Egypt. But Caesar climbs up anyway, and they sit across from each other, each of them perched on a huge paw of the Sphinx.

As Caesar sits there, dumbfounded and bewildered, the little girl babbles on in a monologue reminiscent of *Alice in Wonderland:* she's glad to have helped this "old gentleman" hide himself from the Romans who will eat him, but right now she's all in a twit because the white cat which she brought out to sacrifice to the Sphinx has escaped because a black cat called to it, and it's possible that the black cat could have been the girl's great-great-great-grandmother because *she,* the grandmother, was originally a black kitten of a sacred white cat, and the river Nile made this ancient ancestor his seventh wife (which is why the little girl's hair is wavy: the Nile has waves) and, besides all that, the little girl has great plans for the future if she can manage to solve all of her present problems. For example, since she *is* queen, she is anxious to reclaim her palace in Alexandria, where her brother drove her out, and the first thing that she's going to do is poison the slaves "to see them wriggle." Ordinarily, she'd be home in bed, but the Romans are coming and are going to "eat us all" and so she thought that she'd sacrifice a cat and. . . .Then she looks at the "old gentleman." She asks him why *he* is out on a night like this; *he* is the one who should be at home and be in bed.

Caesar is absolutely fascinated by this little minx. He is overwhelmed by her incoherent fantasies and by her innocent, condescending insolence. And he is more than a little embarrassed to discover that she overheard him talking to the Sphinx, and he is clearly embarrassed to discover that this Sphinx is *not* the Great Sphinx. Why, this Sphinx, says the little girl, is "only a dear little kitten of a Sphinx." In fact, it is her "pet sphinx."

Humbled by this revelation, Caesar becomes, in Shaw's words, "panic-stricken": "Madness, madness!" he cries. "Back to camp — to camp!" The child, however, soothes him, and he in turn dispels her terror of the Romans. He promises to teach her how to prevent Caesar from eating her, and he also promises to teach her how to be a brave woman and a great queen.

Throughout the rest of the act, he plays along with the child; he demonstrates how one assumes courage and how one assumes one's proper role. For example, he insists that Cleopatra act like a queen — that she *become* Queen. As a demonstration, he silences the haughty Ftatateeta (whose name he never does remember correctly; he calls her "Teetatota,"

"Totateeta," and, finally, simply "Tota"). He says that Cleopatra is to discipline her nurse sternly. Such power belongs to Cleopatra; Cleopatra has only to take it. She must command and demand.

Cleopatra is delighted to see her old nurse quail and obey Caesar. Giddy with her new power, she and Caesar romp about the throne room; she vows to "beat somebody...I am a real Queen at last—a real, real Queen!" Meanwhile, Caesar "chops his teeth together," showing her what Caesar will do to her unless she stands boldly before him. If she fears Caesar, she is no true queen, he says, for Caesar recognizes and values pride and courage. Cleopatra must face Caesar and proclaim, "So be it." The young Cleopatra repeats the words, her face white with uncertainty.

The throne room explodes suddenly with the sound of trumpets and wild cries of horror. The Romans have arrived. Caesar places Cleopatra on the steps of the throne and tells her to act like a queen. Then he ascends to the throne, just as the Roman soldiers burst in. They stare in amazement, then draw their swords, and shout, *"Hail, Caesar!"* Cleopatra stares wildly at the old gentleman and "with a great sob of relief, falls into his arms."

ACT II

This second act is less playful than Act I; Shaw's mood is set. He has caught our interest in these wholly new versions of Caesar and Cleopatra, and now he begins with the plot itself. First off, we are treated to a scene of great pageantry. Cleopatra's ten-year-old brother, Ptolemy is descending a grand flight of stairs, preceded by Pothinus, his tutor. The young king is flanked on one side by his tutor (an old, sarcastic eunuch) and on the other side by Achillas (general of Ptolemy's troops). Ptolemy's court receives the young king with reverence as he stands before his throne and begins a formal address. That is, he begins and begins again, and yet begins again with the prompting of his tutor, Theodotus. In essence, he stammeringly tells his court that "the gods" will not allow Cleopatra to "snatch the kingdom from [him] and reign in [his] place." His sister, he says, is aided and abetted by a witch, Ftatateeta, who has cast a spell over Caesar, who now threatens them all. Ptolemy's general is not worried, however; his troops are numerous, and when he tells the court the size of Caesar's legions, the hall fills with hoots of derisive laughter.

The laughter ceases, however, when Caesar is announced. He enters, and his presence throughout this act is, for the most part, very casual and very controlled. Although he is surrounded on all sides by enemies, his calm demeanor is a dramatic contrast to all of the Egyptians' temperamental, nervous apprehension. For example, Caesar pats young King Ptolemy on the head, is introduced to the king's chief attendants, and then comes directly to the point: he is "badly in want of money," and the Egyptians owe him money — a "lawful debt due to Rome by Egypt, contracted by the king's deceased father to the Triumvirate." This is daring melodrama: Caesar has come into the enemy's central court — not to conquer, but to collect an overdue bill.

The king's guardian is aghast. The bill which Caesar demands is exorbitant: "the king's taxes have not been collected for a year." Caesar has news for them: his officers have been collecting taxes all morning. Pothinus taunts Caesar that a conqueror should have better things to do than collect overdue bills; Caesar disagrees. "Taxes," he says, "are a chief business of the conqueror of the world." Furthermore, he adds, this matter of who *really* rules Egypt should be settled once and for all. To the court's astonishment, he calls for Cleopatra, who is led in by Ftatateeta.

As a balance and a contrast to this matter of the businesslike tax collecting, young Ptolemy and Cleopatra have a verbal and physical battle for the throne, and then they engage in a similar battle for Caesar's favor — which Cleopatra wins. She is magnificent in her decision that it is far worthier to sit beside the mighty Caesar than alone on an Egyptian throne; besides, she does not fear Caesar. Ptolemy does. She urges Caesar to eat him: "Eat my husband...he is afraid." Momentarily, Caesar is caught off-guard by this revelation, but accepts the Egyptian custom, a concept which Caesar's stuffy British attendant, Britannus, cannot bear to even think about.

Achillas can take no more; he threatens Caesar. After all, he, Achillas, is general of the Roman occupation here in Alexandria. Caesar is unconcerned. Pothinus also tries to frighten Caesar, reminding him that Caesar is *not* invincible. Why only a few weeks ago, he says, "Caesar was flying for his life before Pompey." Caesar's attending officer, Rufio, bites his beard at this reminder, but "Caesar sits as comfortably as if he were at breakfast, and the cat were clamoring for a piece of Finnan-haddie." (Such pointed, unexpected bits of Shavian whimsy occur continually throughout the play; they are lost to the theatergoer. For this reason, Shaw's plays are always worth reading *and* viewing.) Caesar's calmness is questioned by even Cleopatra at this point; is he truly unafraid? "I shall not go away," he tells her, "until you are Queen." To Rufio's dismay, Caesar dismisses the Egyptians, even the "Roman army of occupation." Ptolemy's guardian is confused; *he* should be the one dismissing everyone—not Caesar. In a desperate maneuver to break Caesar's cool exterior, he calls forth a trim, handsome Roman of about forty; it is Lucius Septimus. Here is Pompey's slayer, Pothinus boasts; were it not for this hero, perhaps Caesar would not be alive today.

Caesar is appalled at Lucius' barbarian sense of honor. Clearly, Lucius would have slain Caesar for the Egyptians had Pompey been victorious at Pharsalia. Caesar's moral code cannot condone such acts. Truly, he himself kills—but when Caesar kills, he kills with "a wise severity, a necessary protection to the commonwealth, and a duty of statesmanship." What Lucius has done is worthy only of a wolf. He sends him away—again to Rufio's fearful warnings.

Cleopatra asks if she is to go too, and Caesar tells her that she must do as she pleases; she is free. But he would like her to stay. She does, and Caesar commands "Tota" to fetch Egyptian women to attend Cleopatra. Ftatateeta balks, and Cleopatra threatens to throw her into the Nile and thereby poison the crocodiles. Caesar feigns horror at such a threat—to which Cleopatra reassures him that all will be well when he ceases to be so sentimental. "You will soon learn to govern," she says sagely. Hmmm, he muses, he may have to eat this child yet. Then he announces that he must make plans. Cleopatra begs for his time, but he insists that immediate plans are necessary for his troops.

He commands Rufio to burn the ships in the west harbor and, with the ships in the east harbor, his forces will seize Pharos, the island with the lighthouse. Half their men will hold the beach and the wharf outside the palace. Rufio thinks such orders are insane, but he leaves anyway. Very shortly, Ptolemy's tutor rushes in, breathless: the library of Alexandria is in flames; "the first of the seven wonders of the world perishes." Caesar is unperturbed by Theodotus' pleas for mercy; it is better, says Caesar, that Egyptians should live life than dream their lives away in books. He does not fear that history may fail to record his death; death itself will accomplish that deed. And as for "the memory of mankind" ablaze in smoke, "it is a shameful memory." If the past is being destroyed, as Theodotus claims, then Caesar will "build the future with its ruins." He spurns this so-called tutor to a king who valued Pompey's head "no more than a shepherd values an onion" and who now pleads "for a few sheepskins scrawled with errors."

The act ends with a final bit of comedy. As Cleopatra helps dress Caesar in his armor, she bursts out laughing when he removes his oak wreath and she sees that he is bald. He reminds her that just as she doesn't like to be reminded that she is very young (even though she is sixteen), Caesar doesn't like to "be reminded that [he is]—[pause] middle-aged." They agree to add ten years to her age and subtract ten from his.

As Caesar makes ready to leave, he counsels Cleopatra once again not to be afraid; she "must learn to look on battles." Rufio looks at the west harbor; the Egyptians are "crawling...like locusts." This was, of course, Caesar's strategy: "the library will keep them busy whilst we seize the lighthouse." Cleopatra waves her scarf after Caesar. "Goodby," she calls, "goodbye, dear Caesar. Come back safe. Goodbye." Once again, she is a child, waving goodbye to, in this case, someone who is like one of the gods, someone who is like no one she has ever met before.

ACT III

Caesar and his forces have seized the lighthouse on Pharos island and are now faced with the problem of keeping the Egyptians from using the five-mile stone breakfront, connecting the island to the mainland, to their advantage. Meanwhile, back on the pier of the mainland, a sentinel stops Ftatateeta and Apollodorus the Sicilian. Apollodorus resents being questioned; already he and Ftatateeta have passed three sentinels without being interrogated. "Is this Roman discipline?" he asks. The sentinel is not amused, and the scene that follows is filled with colorful, spirited comedy. Apollodorus is foppish, and Shaw gives him a good measure of double-edged rejoinders. *He* is no "carpet merchant"; he is a patrician and a keeper of "a temple of the arts." He chooses "beautiful things for beautiful queens"; his motto is "Art for Art's sake." In contrast, Ftatateeta is impatient with the sentinel in *her* own way. She would stab the sentinel, "the little Roman reptile" who called her a "piece of Egyptian crockery."

Cleopatra hears the fracas from an upper palace window and comes down to silence it. She sees the rich rolls of carpets and has an idea. According to orders, no one is allowed to row out to the lighthouse, but Cleopatra has learned from Caesar that boldness is a queen's best virtue. Thus, she and Ftatateeta return to the palace, roll Cleopatra in one of the carpets and, well concealed, she is carefully carried out.

Apollodorus feigns an alarm that the Egyptians are about to recapture the lighthouse, and the ruse works. The soldiers scatter, and Apollodorus convinces the sentinel to let him load the carpet onto his boat and row out. Only after it is too late to prevent Apollodorus from reaching the lighthouse does the sentinel pay attention to the prayers of Ftatateeta; as she asks the gods to protect her "nursling," the sentinel realizes that Cleopatra is rolled inside the rug. That explains the great care that was taken in loading and Apollodorus' extreme concern for the carpet's "worth."

The scene shifts then to the tower of the lighthouse. Rufio, Caesar's general, is taking a break from the morning's fighting and is lunching on a helmetful of dates. Caesar is gazing out at the sea; he fears that his plan was rash and "boyish": "We shall be beaten." This is the first time, he confesses, that he has "run an avoidable risk." He says further that he "should not have come to Egypt."

At this point, Britannus rushes in with what he thinks is very good news. A bag containing all the letters which passed between Pompey's army and Achillas' army of occupation has been captured. According to Britannus, the letters contain the names of every man "who plotted against Caesar since he crossed the Rubicon." To Britannus' astonishment, Caesar picks up the heavy bag and heaves it over the parapet and into the sea. At least three years would be wasted, he says, sorting through this mail and making up an "enemies list." He scorns his aide's puny British mind and its petty, contemptible concepts of honor and warfare.

Apollodorus enters and greets Caesar: he has a present from "the Queen of Queens." Caesar has no time for gifts at present; he tells Apollodorus to leave. Unfortunately, Apollodorus cannot leave; "some fool" dropped a huge, heavy leather bag over the top of the parapet, and it hit the prow of his boat. Apollodorus was barely able to save himself and his exquisite Persian carpet, which is below, waiting to be presented to Caesar. Caesar is interested and intrigued when he learns that the carpet contains pigeons' eggs and crystal goblets. Even the normally gruff Rufio is interested. The total absurdity of their dining on pigeons' eggs and sipping from crystal goblets—in the midst of what well may be their last battle—is too great a temptation. Thus Apollodorus orders it to be brought up, and a rattling, unsound chain and crane are employed and, accompanied by heavy heaving and cries of anxiety from Apollodorus, the carpet is finally swung around and deposited at Caesar's feet. Rufio is wary; who knows what is truly coiled inside the rug? He sees a movement and is ready to run his sword through the carpet when Caesar thrusts a hand inside, and Cleopatra emerges, gasping for air: "I'm smothered," she says. "A man stood on me in the boat; and a great sack of something fell upon me out of the sky; and then the boat sank; and then I was swung up into the air and bumped down." She is breathless, as is Britannus; he is horrified by her presence, and he tells Caesar that she absolutely cannot stay "without the companionship of some matron." He may be only a barely civilized Briton of 43 B.C., but Shaw clearly intends to satirize here the prudish English temperament that, even then, insisted on everything being "terribly proper."

Caesar is not pleased that Cleopatra has smuggled herself inside his fortress. He has troops to command, and when Cleopatra insists that soldiers' lives are worthless, he tells her candidly that her "life matters little here"; in fact, at present, she is the only one who is concerned with *her* welfare. And he is not happy to learn that she *cannot* return—even if she would agree to. Apollodorus' boat is sunk. There is little time for planning; a great tumult is heard, and Britannus announces that the Egyptians have landed from the west harbor. Rufio realizes instantly that they are "caught like rats in a trap."

This is not precisely the case. Caesar realizes what is possible: he has ships in the east harbor. If he can reach them, he can defend his men who are caught on the barricade. Thus he makes ready to dive off, promising to carry Cleopatra on his back, "like a dolphin." The "terribly proper" Britannus is horrified at the impromptu turn of events: he is a Briton, not a fish. *He* is staying behind and he begs one last word with Caesar: "Do not let yourself be seen in the fashionable part of Alexandria until [you have] changed clothes."

Caesar plunges over, followed by the screaming, excited Cleopatra (who is tossed over by Rufio), and then Rufio springs off the parapet, instructing Britannus to "hold the fort" — Caesar will not forget him. Britannus is ever so confident that all will go swimmingly; venting his excitement, he cheers his comrades on: "Hip, hip, hip, hurrah!"

ACT IV

This act begins five months later. Cleopatra, attended by a number of young attendants (including two of her favorites, Charmian and Iras), is listening to a slave girl playing the harp. Cleopatra muses; she would like to learn to play the harp. Her court musician answers her that he can teach her to play it well. She saucily replies that he had better; if she happens to strike a false note, he will be flogged. Cleopatra is no longer kittenish; she now seems to be a full-grown, mature "cat" — a fact which will be confirmed shortly when Charmian teasingly refers to the fact that Cleopatra is a *woman* now.

Cleopatra is bored; she would like a story or some news. Iras says that Pothinus, Ptolemy's guardian, has been trying — unsuccessfully, so far — to bribe Ftatateeta. Cleopatra wrathfully answers them all that she is quite aware of the bribes offered in the palace. Charmian agrees and sassily says that Cleopatra's condoning this practice is merely in imitation of Caesar's well-known clemency. She and Iras would like Caesar to be back in Rome. His presence has made Cleopatra "prosy and serious and learned and philosophical." This impertinence infuriates Cleopatra; she is no puppet of Caesar. Only she herself is her mistress. She demands that Pothinus be brought to her immediately; she will find out why he has been trying to bribe Ftatateeta.

When Pothinus is brought in, Cleopatra demands to know what scheme he is planning. He stammers onto another subject: he is only a poor prisoner, and she is a child too young to understand wisdom. The ladies all titter, and Cleopatra dismisses them, all of them, which does *not* please Ftatateeta, who accuses Cleopatra of becoming "what these Romans call a New Woman." When Pothinus and Cleopatra are alone, Pothinus acknowledges that Cleopatra has changed. He had hoped to trick the "little nursery kitten." Now he realizes that he cannot.

Cleopatra decides that it is time that her brother's guardian realize that *she* is queen. Furthermore, she is no paramour of Caesar. Caesar is kind to her, but that is all; they are not lovers. By nature, Caesar is kind to her in the same way that he is kind to everyone, even dogs and children. This same kindness extends even to his servant Britannus and, likewise (Shaw is tweaking English pride again here), just as kind as he is to his horse. Cleopatra confesses that she has tried to make Caesar jealous — and failed. She loves another Roman, anyway, a man who slew her sister's husband and returned her father's throne to him; this man (Mark Antony), she says, "can love and hate"; she can hurt him, and he can hurt her. Caesar knows of her infatuation for this man; he has even promised to send Antony to Egypt to please Cleopatra. Pothinus is truly puzzled; he does not understand Caesar. He states that Caesar will be defeated; Cleopatra, of course, emphatically denies this. Caesar will defeat her brother's troops, and Cleopatra will finally be queen. Caesar cannot fail. He has accomplished the impossible with only two legions. Already, eighteen legions hasten to reinforce him. She exits, and Ftatateeta enters and hears Pothinus vow that while he lives, Cleopatra "shall never rule."

The scene changes; Caesar, fresh from his bath, is dining with Rufio. Shortly, Pothinus is admitted; he has come to tell Caesar that Cleopatra is waiting for him to leave. Her chief concern is not Caesar's presence, but his absence, for only then can she rule as Egypt's monarch. Pothinus begins his confidence, but he is stopped by Cleopatra's entrance. She is enraged to see him confiding in Caesar. Teasingly, Caesar not only dismisses Pothinus, but he also frees him — in celebration of Caesar's birthday. This "mercy" further angers Cleopatra; she does not trust the man. Pothinus then tells Caesar of Cleopatra's politics, and while Cleopatra protests and proclaims Pothinus to be a liar, Caesar listens. He finds such news very natural; some may call it treachery, but treachery is natural, and it is as futile to *resent* treachery as it is to resent a chilly wind or a dark night. Caesar then decides to personally escort Pothinus past the guards.

While they are gone, Cleopatra threatens her nurse; if Pothinus leaves the palace again, "never see my face again." She strikes Ftatateeta across the mouth. "Strike his life out as I strike his name from your lips...Kill, kill, kill him." Ftatateeta swears to do so, "showing all her teeth": "The dog shall perish."

When Caesar returns with Apollodorus, their conversation turns to the possibility of Caesar's conquering all of Africa for Cleopatra and Caesar to rule. Apollodorus is fascinated by the idea. A name, however, would be required for this new nation. Several are suggested, but none of them pleases Cleopatra. She suggests that the Nile itself—literally—name the new nation. The Major-Domo, who has been attending the dinner party, is asked to attend to the details of Cleopatra's request, and he exits "as if he had received the most matter-of-fact order." Cleopatra then tells them all that the Nile will give them an answer, but they must all say, in unison, "send us thy voice, Father Nile." They do—and hear "the death cry of a man in mortal terror and agony." Caesar feels instinctively that murder has been committed, and he instructs Apollodorus to leave and find out what has actually happened. Ftatateeta enters, flushed, and this time it is Rufio who feels instinctively that he knows what has taken place. His hunch is confirmed when Cleopatra flings her arms around her nurse's neck, and she kisses her repeatedly, then tears off her exquisite queenly jewels and heaps them on her nurse.

Caesar asks Cleopatra in all earnestness to tell him what she knows of all this; she, of course, denies knowing anything: "I am innocent...I have been here with you all the time. How can I know what has happened?" She tries to cajole Caesar with tears and feigned concern, but she fails. Thus she continues to swear that she has not betrayed Caesar. His answer to her is cold and cutting: "I know that. I have not trusted you." In other words, one can only be betrayed by a person whom one has trusted.

Rufio announces at this point that the town has gone mad. The mob means to tear the palace down and drive them all into the sea. Caesar still has not fathomed who has been murdered, and so Lucius tells him: it is Pothinus, the guardian of young Ptolemy, the man whom Caesar just set free and accompanied past the guards.

Cleopatra is cornered. She confesses that the order to kill Pothinus came from her, from "the Queen of Egypt." She boasts that *she* is "not Julius Caesar the dreamer, who allows every slave to insult him." Lucius agrees that Cleopatra's order was right; in turn, Apollodorus, Britannus, and Rufio agree with Lucius: Cleopatra was right to give the order to kill Pothinus. Caesar reflects on their mutual agreement. Perhaps, he tells them, only a man who has conquered the world or has been crucified by it would disagree with them. Thus, he says, in effect, now the populace demands vengeance. Throughout history, murder has bred murder, "always in the name of right and honor and peace." Now Cleopatra must defend herself; Caesar is only a dreamer.

Cleopatra is terrified at such a prospect. Rufio tells his general that the enemy is at the gate." Caesar is tempted to "open [his] hand and let [them] all sink into the flood." Clearly, to the Egyptians, the Romans are a nest of assassins. Yesterday, they clamored for Pompey's head; today, Caesar's is ripe. Asked if he despairs, Caesar answers with "infinite pride": "He who has never hoped can never despair." Lucius offers his services — and a piece of good news: the reinforcements are on the march, which means that every soldier in the city will be trying to thwart their advance across the Nile. The city is defended by only old women and children.

Caesar makes Lucius an officer and begins making military plans. Cleopatra tries to divert him, but he dismisses her: "I am busy now, child, busy...be good and patient." Arrogantly, Rufio tells Cleopatra that she played for Caesar and lost; women *always* lose, he boasts. Moreover, her assassin bungled his work. He should have stabbed Pothinus in the throat. Retaliating, Cleopatra asks Rufio why he assumes that a *man* killed Pothinus. Almost simultaneously, Rufio sees Ftatateeta. Cleopatra, however, does not notice Rufio's glance. Beware, she warns him: "You who dare make the Queen of Egypt a fool before Caesar." Rufio leaves then, and Cleopatra hears repeatedly "Hail, Caesar! Hail, hail!" Suddenly frightened, she calls out to Ftatateeta. In a panic when her old nurse does not come, she pulls the curtains where Ftatateeta was praying before the white altarstone of Ra. Ftatateeta is lying dead on the altar; her throat has been cut, and her blood flows over the white stone.

ACT V

The setting is a festival, and all kinds of military pageantry fill the stage. Caesar's galley, ready to sail, is rigged abundantly with flowers. Six months have passed. Apollodorus and Belzanor meet and discuss events which have occurred during this time. Among them, young King Ptolemy has been drowned. Currently, Caesar is buying idols in the marketplace and "settling the Jewish question."

Shortly, Caesar arrives. He announces that the hour of his farewell to Egypt has arrived. Rufio reminds him that he has not appointed a governor to rule Egypt, and so Caesar suggests that Rufio assume the post. Rufio is incredulous. He is only the "son of a freedman"; he is "Caesar's shield." Rufio does not accept the governorship with much happiness. He fears what may happen to Caesar when his general returns to Rome: "without your shield [Rufio]," he tells Caesar, there is danger; in Rome, "there are too many daggers." Philosophically, Caesar says that he has never much cared to think about dying; almost jokingly, he comments, "I had rather be killed." Shaw was aware, of course, of the heavy dramatic irony that he was inserting in these lines.

Before Caesar leaves, Cleopatra enters, dressed starkly in black. Caesar asks why, and she accuses Rufio of murdering her nurse. Caesar is puzzled. Rufio says that if he were to meet a hungry lion, he would kill it; else, the lion would eat him. Caesar agrees with Rufio's metaphor. The lion should be killed — without malice. Cleopatra had a tigress that killed at Cleopatra's bidding; Rufio killed that tigress — without malice. The slaying was a natural slaying. Caesar feels no horror at it. He is, though, he confesses, "sorry for that poor Totateeta." At this, Cleopatra cannot help from laughing. Truly, Caesar tells her, she is still a child. And the two tease one another about which is the greater baby: she, or he (who has never been able to remember Ftatateeta's name). On this loving, laughing note, Caesar bids Cleopatra farewell, promising to send her a beautiful present from Rome — a man, "Roman from head to heel and Roman of the noblest; not old and ripe...not lean in the arms and not cold in the heart... nor hiding a bald head under his conqueror's laurels." In short, he promises her Mark Antony. He will remember her always, even though he is sure that they will never meet again. They kiss goodbye, and as Cleopatra waves her handkerchief, and Caesar's ship beings to move away, the curtains close, the Roman soldiers all drawing their swords and proclaiming "Hail, Caesar!"

In this final act, when Rufio, Caesar, and Cleopatra discuss the killing of Ftatateeta, Shaw summed up what he believed made a good ruler. Already we have seen him characterize Caesar as being "a great talker and a politician," a soldier and a conqueror. Caesar was favored by the gods; Ra told us that. Caesar's adversary, Pompey, was not favored by the gods because "he talked of law and duty and other matters that concerned not a mere human worm." Caesar, in contrast, had "wit enough [to] become what he could. The gods detest boasting, just as they detest enslavement." Nowhere in the play do we see Caesar seriously boast to other men; likewise, he is scorned by his own men because of his clemency. This play, Ra told us, was to be presented "for the good of [our] souls." Caesar sought out Pompey to destroy him and his immoral code. Pompey was killed and, by accident, Caesar encountered Cleopatra. For a few brief moments in history, their paths crossed. And when they parted, each was wiser, even though Caesar could not have foreseen that he was returning to a Roman senate that was filled with men who believed and acted very much like Pompey. Ironically, Rufio, Caesar's "shield," foresaw this possibility.

Originally, the Egyptians (especially Belzanor) hoped to use Cleopatra to seduce Caesar; this proved to be ultimately an impossibility. Caesar's codes were new and revolutionary. He defied past codes of conquerors. Ironically, Cleopatra could have easily seduced Pompey. Caesar, in this play, is a new kind of hero — wry, ironic, and not bound by old formulas and outdated dogmas. When the library at Alexandria burned, it furnished a diversion to save Caesar's forces. As for the books in the library, they were worthless, says Caesar; they are history texts, sheepskins scrawled with errors. If the past is being destroyed, he will build the future on the ruins of the past. Men like Caesar are rare, Shaw implies; he died too soon. Men like Pompey abound and beget; twenty centuries have passed, and men still "speak and live, no worse and no better, no wiser and no sillier." To Shaw, ignorance is vice. He hoped, a little, to remedy this with his plays, where he could dress his ideas and expound on them and entertain at the same time. He hoped that his wit would ignite and destroy Victorian humbug and shock prudish sensibility into new visions of what mankind might be.

Caesar is one of Shaw's finest dramatic creations. He is old, and he has achieved a great deal, but he is still humanly flawed with vanity, occasional self-doubt, and innocence; yet, when tested, he has a spine of unyielding principle. His wit is razor-keen, and yet his comic sense is amusing when he gives it rein. He is able to teach Cleopatra a great deal about governing her people before he leaves her; he creates a fierce independence within her which she never had before. And, at the play's conclusion, she is able to match wits with Caesar. It is a fulfilling evening to read this play, just as it is to see it performed on stage; to do both is to begin to realize the unmatched theatrical genius of Shaw.

QUESTIONS FOR REVIEW

1. What does Ra mean by the "old Rome and the new Rome"? How should one parallel this with today's changing values?

2. Contrast Caesar and Pompey.

3. How do the Egyptians hope to use their queen to conquer Caesar if he is an "old man"?

4. Characterize Ftatateeta.

5. Describe Caesar's initial fascination with Cleopatra.

6. According to Caesar, why has he come to Ptolemy's palace in Alexandria.

7. What is the relationship between Ptolemy and Cleopatra?

8. Caesar reacts differently to the deaths of Pothinus and Ftatateeta. Account for each of his reactions.

9. What is the quintessence of Caesar's moral and military code?

10. Is the play ultimately pessimistic or optimistic? Explain.

SELECTED BIBLIOGRAPHY

Duffin, H. C. *The Quintessence of Bernard Shaw*. London, 1920.

Fuller, Edmund. *George Bernard Shaw, Critic of Western Morale*. New York, 1950.

Howe, P. O. *Bernard Shaw*. London, 1915.

Irvine, William. *The Universe of GBS*. New York, 1949.

Kronenberger, Louis, ed. *George Bernard Shaw: A Critical Survey*. Cleveland and New York, 1953.

Mencken, H. L. *George Bernard Shaw: His Plays*. Boston, 1905.

Rattray, R. F. *Bernard Shaw: A Chronicle and an Introduction*. London, 1951.

Skimpole, Herbert. *Bernard Shaw: The Man and His Work*. London, 1918.

Strauss, E. *Bernard Shaw, Art, and Socialism*. London, 1942.

Ward, A. C. *Bernard Shaw*. London, 1951.

NOTES